★ THE ★
LEADERSHIP
CAMPAIGN

SCOTT MILLER
AND DAVID MOREY

THE LEADERSHIP CAMPAIGN

10 POLITICAL STRATEGIES TO WIN AT YOUR CAREER AND PROPEL YOUR BUSINESS TO VICTORY

CAREER
PRESS

Pompton Plains, N.J.

THE LEADERSHIP CAMPAIGN
EDITED BY PATRICIA KOT
TYPESET BY KARA KUMPEL
Cover design by Ty Nowicki
Button images by Michael McDonald/123rf
Printed in the U.S.A.

To order this title, please call toll-free 1-800-CAREER-1 (NJ and Canada: 201-848-0310) to order using VISA or MasterCard, or for further information on books from Career Press.

The Career Press, Inc.
12 Parish Drive
Wayne, NJ 07470
www.careerpress.com

Library of Congress Cataloging-in-Publication Data
CIP Data Available Upon Request.

To Denise, Tyler, and Brett. To the late Steven Jobs and the very lively Mike Murray of Apple Computer for setting us on the insurgent path to leadership.

–SM

To Xie Zheng, who helps me be a better leader and person every day. To Sue, the best sister a brother can have. And to our clients, who teach us more than we can ever teach them.

–DM

CONTENTS

PREFACE

The point of this book is to teach you how to develop the leadership skills needed in a changing and challenging business environment. The principles of leadership we preach are those of successful insurgents and revolutionaries in business, politics, and warfare. In the Information Age in which we all live and work, insurgents hold the advantage over incumbents. The status quo in business leadership that developed over the past hundred years simply no longer cuts it. The tried-and-true has been tried and tried and is no longer true.

So the further premise of this book is that the model of leadership used by most organizations is broken. We need new strategies, different approaches, new training, and new ways of communicating. All of these are aspects of the "new leadership," which, it turns out, is not new to us. Back in the 1980s, we called it "change leadership" in the model we developed for Steven Jobs and Mike Murray at Apple Computer. Today, that term is more relevant than ever. In our work and in our lives, change is in control of the dialogue.

In 2004, we wrote *The Underdog Advantage* as a primer on the insurgent forces, which were (and still are, even more intensely) disrupting business, politics, and warfare. In ten actionable steps, *The Leadership Campaign* will show you how to use the insurgent political model as a strategy to succeed in your career and help your project, team, or company succeed in today's complex and competitive markets. This insurgent model is the best path to the change leadership that is required today.

Step by step, we'll go through the basics of "The Leadership Campaign." You'll see that it is laid out just like a political campaign, from beginning through victory party. This is not just an effective metaphor. It is a framework that builds success and gets the win for a group or an individual leader by keeping the entire team's focus lasered-in on results that *must* be won by its self-defined "Election Day."

We offer here the ten fundamental steps in developing success—just as we have experienced it and have seen it in countless political and business campaigns, and for countless candidates, CEOs, and CEOs in the making. Each step is an important element in the development of more focus, energy, and effective strategies and tactics for your company, team, or your own career. So, no skipping!

It's the White House or the Outhouse

Maybe we're adrenaline junkies. But the White House-or-Outhouse stakes of the political campaign have always had a grip on us. You get 50.1% on the first Tuesday after the first Monday in November, or you go home. There are a lot of tense nights and a lot of *all*-nighters working to build that winning .1%. There are a lot of mornings you wake up with that dull ache in the pit of your stomach, with that creeping sense that you're just not going to make it there. You play on a motley team of experts, Big Data nerds, issue wonks, scruffy field organizers, slick ad people, and gruff managers, all of whom share that one commitment: the win, the whole win, and nothing but the win.

The adrenaline rush, the ache, the fear, and the hope are all concentrated into every campaign and often stirred together into any one day. If you can't take that upside-down, loop-dee-loop roller coaster ride, then you're not cut out for politics.

In the mid-1980s, facing off against the towering IBM business juggernaut, Apple Computer was the pesky insurgent versus the seemingly untouchable decades-old incumbent. Steven Jobs had the idea that an insurgent political strategy and its nothing-but-the-win culture might be just what it would take to win.

Back in 1984, we were making a very nice living as political campaign consultants, managing fifteen or twenty U.S. campaigns as well as the campaigns of democratic revolutionaries around the world. Then Jobs invited us to lunch. "You guys know something we don't know," he told us. "You people do strategy differently than people do in business. You play for all the marbles— White House or Outhouse. And I think you develop a little sharper plans and sharper elbows than corporate strategists. I'd like you to think about our competition with IBM as if it were a political campaign."

Jobs was asking us to apply what we knew about political campaigning to leadership, marketing, and communications in business. That struck us as pretty ironic because, back then, political candidates all over the world hired us to apply to their *political* campaigns what we knew about *business* communication and marketing strategy.

And so it took Steve Jobs to nudge us in the ribs—talk about "sharp elbows"!—and tell us that we could take to business leadership everything we knew about political campaigning. Our work with him in the mid-1980s was the first time we had applied our political strategy to a business campaign.

To be specific, Jobs and his brilliant chief marketing officer, Mike Murray, helped us develop what we now call the Insurgent Model—essentially the opposition of change leaders to bigness leaders.

Since working with Apple, we have worked with The Coca-Cola Company, The Home Depot, Google, American Express, McDonald's, Microsoft, Johnson & Johnson, Verizon, News Corp, Miller Brewing, HBO, Samuel Adams, TPG, Nike, Visa, General Electric, The Walt Disney Company, and many others, including more than a few start-ups and upstarts.

Notice that many of our clients are very successful companies and most, in fact, are incumbents. Well, even the most successful corporations in the world face difficult challenges and awesome changes in today's turbulent business environment. When they are confronted by genuine disruption, that's when they tend to call on us. What we tell them, first and foremost, is that *they* need to disrupt their market or their own status quo. *They* need to do what's being done to them—and do it better and more urgently.

Disrupting markets. Disrupting the status quo. These are the specialties of the insurgent political leader and the insurgent political campaign. Steven Jobs did not steer us wrong. For over thirty years now, we've found that insurgent political model to be as effective in business as it is in politics.

Now, we freely admit that to this toaster, everything looks like sliced pumpernickel. Yes, we apply our campaign model to everything we do—to short business projects; to whole-hog, top-to-bottom reinvention of corporate vision and objectives; and to the careers of individual executives at every level. Whatever the leadership situation, we apply the model because it works.

The two deficiencies that dilute, contaminate, and generally muck up business strategies and business projects are the same two deficiencies that stall business leadership careers.

1. **Lack of focus.** Misidentifying the problem or the opportunity creates vague objectives or objectives that are just plain wrong. So does failure to understand the entire battlefield, failure to laser-in on just the targets you need to hit, and failure to put together the right team for the challenge. Any of these deficiencies in focus invite drift. Your project—or your company—meanders off course; your own career starts to sputter.

2. **Lack of urgency.** How many corporate projects actually reach their stated goals? In our experience, the number is about 8%. Project managers and teams don't take this lying down. About 92% of them respond by moving the goal line or otherwise scramble to diminish the expectations of stakeholders.

And how many corporate managers and CEOs fail to reach their leadership potential? In our experience, about 92%. They console themselves with their fairly big bucks, their next-to-primo parking space, and their proximity to the top dog (i.e., just beneath).

The Leadership Campaign is about providing focus and urgency to your project, your team, your company, and your own career. One hundred percent of the time, these two things are precisely what you need. Ninety-two percent of companies (which means yours, most likely) don't have them.

The Leadership Campaign is about the most important unmet need today in business, politics, the military, academia, and the arts. It's all about leadership.

In a world of change, the outcome of successful leadership is constant. It is the rise and triumph of teams, companies, countries, and individuals. The components of successful leadership, however, are in continual change as the environment for leadership changes. In today's environment, markets have changed, competitors have changed, employee attitudes have changed, and consumers have changed. What *hasn't* changed are most business strategies and management strategies.

What also hasn't changed is the scarcity of real leaders. We may call our boss a leader, but chances are she/he isn't one. They're just the boss.

The requirements for today's leaders are vastly different from what they were ten or even five years ago. In fact, the requirements keep changing in the change environment in which we all live and work.

We keep hearing that innovation is the thing that all businesses (and governments) need most today. But you never unlock the potential for innovation without great leadership.

In any given local, state, or national election, the pundits may say jobs or immigration or foreign policy or taxes are the most important issue. But to the voters, leadership is the issue. The primacy of that issue never changes. Leadership is, was, and will always be *the* issue.

Do you want to be a leader? Do you want to be a more effective leader? Do you want to create a change-leader culture within your team or company?

We have the strategy for you. We've learned from the best: Jobs, Aquino, Gates, Kim, Gorsky, Murdoch, Milken, Keough, Iger, Zyman, Bonderman, Knight, Roberts, Goizueta, and many more.

We developed our Campaign Model by bonding what we learn in politics to what we learn in business. The result is a new leadership model: Change Leadership. It is simple, clear, focused, and energizing as hell. Plus, as the great Henry Kissinger used to say about whatever State Department strategy he was promoting at the time, "This has the added benefit of being true."

✪ Step 1 ✪
DECIDE to Run

Why are you running? What do you believe? Commit!

Why Are You Running?

In 1980 with the Iranian hostage crisis, out-of-control interest rates, and a general "malaise" afflicting the electorate, incumbent Jimmy Carter was losing the faith of the people. At the deepest point of the president's swoon, Senator Edward Kennedy came to the podium of historic Faneuil Hall in Boston to announce that he would enter the presidential campaign against Carter. This electrified the press. Most of the mainstream journalists still remembered and longed for the magic of JFK's Camelot. The campaign left that launch pad like a NASA Atlas rocket. But the end came sooner than the first primary. The unraveling of the "Teddy in '80" campaign arrived dramatically

17

in what should have been a softball prime time interview by CBS re-
porter Roger Mudd. It came down to one question that left Kennedy
stumbling and stammering. "Senator," Mudd asked. "Why are you
running for president?"

All companies have bosses, but big companies have them by
the boatload. They have CEOs and presidents and general managers, executive VPs, VPs, directors, and on and on. Lots of bosses.
But very few companies—especially the big ones—have leaders.

Does yours? Does it have true leaders, visionary leaders, inspi-
rational leaders?

We recognize that not everybody wants to be a leader. Some
people want to follow. They may doubt their own ability to lead.
They may like the warmth of the herd around them. And they
may not like the feeling of untrodden grass underfoot. Not everybody wants to be a leader.

There's also a significant difference between bossing and leading. And it's true that a lot of people get to be the boss by following, not leading. They follow the current boss very, very closely, essentially slip-streaming her through the last several years of
her tenure. They follow the boss's footsteps and then follow the
path the boss would have trod, if the boss hadn't taken the package and retired to the condo in Hilton Head. Chances are that
boss followed just behind the one just ahead of her.

If you want to be a boss, there's always a well-beaten path to
follow. At most companies, the name of that path is "We Do It
This Way, Because That's the Way We've Always Done It." The
path is aptly named, particularly in the case of market leaders,
long-term market incumbents, and those companies that try to
emulate the market incumbents by playing what is essentially an
adult version of follow-the-leader.

Incumbents are very superstitious about their success. We
say they are heritage-driven, because they expect the strategies,

approaches, and rituals of the past to carry them to success in the future. In today's markets, that's like driving in the Monaco Grand Prix while looking only in your rearview mirror.

Every day, the business pages deliver the obituaries of the former market incumbents, one after the other. Most have sputtered to a stop rather than crashed in flames. But an end is an end just the same, and in the case of incumbents, it is the inevitable result of heritage-driven strategy. When the bosses tell themselves they tried everything to avert failure, what they really mean is that they tried everything to avert failure they had always tried before. What finally killed their enterprise is the new environment, which calls for new ideas, new approaches, and new leadership.

Do you want to be a boss or do you want to be a leader? That's the central question of this book. We're talking to people who want to be leaders. While bosses at incumbent companies are generally heritage driven, real leaders—by which we necessarily mean insurgent leaders—are vision driven. They lead toward a new idea and into new territory that they envision, but where footprints to follow are few to none.

If there's one thing that distinguishes these new leaders from old bosses, it is their attitude toward change. Incumbents hate change. Hell, if you're number one, why would you want anything to change? They hate disruption, right to the core of their corporate being. But insurgents love change. Change means molecules in motion. Change means opportunity.

Throughout this book, we'll also show you how to wring every last ounce of opportunity out of any project or objective in your company. The strategies and tactics that create successful projects are based on the same principles that drive leadership. They're all about driving for the win and never, ever doing anything just because "that's the way we've always done it."

In the leadership model we developed for Steven Jobs and Mike Murray at Apple, we contrasted two kinds of leadership: *bigness leadership vs. change leadership.*

- ✪ **Bigness leadership** is the leadership of the incumbent and is the norm of leadership culture at the great majority of companies, most of which follow the leading incumbent in strategy and style. Bigness leaders love size, share, and gross profit—whatever is about bigness.

- ✪ **Change leadership** values speed and mobility over size. It's all about change and disruption. Change leaders want to create marketplace value. They figure share will follow. They focus on net, because that's a better metric for evaluating true marketplace value. You can't cut your way to sustainable net profit.

- ✪ **Bigness leaders** like formality in business processes and bureaucracy driving the organization. Formality and bureaucracy are like the orthodox rituals of many religions. They are intended to promise that what was will be.

- ✪ **Change leaders** are informal in demeanor, organization, and development of strategy. We aren't talking about "casual Friday" every day or sushi in the cafeteria. We are talking about a bias toward loose organization and flexible strategies. Change leaders organize organically around the challenge inherent in their business vision. What works is what works—until it doesn't work.

- ✪ To the **incumbent leader**, disruption is disturbing. It's what happens to them, not what they cause to happen.

- ✪ To the **insurgent leader**, disruption is the central business process.

We want to teach you to be an insurgent, a change leader, because that's the style of leadership that succeeds in today's business, political, military, and information age. In an environment in which change is in control of the dialogue, insurgents hold the winning cards against incumbents everywhere.

Learn to Love Change

If you want to become a leader today, whether you are leading a short-term project, a startup, or a global corporation, we already know the theme of your campaign for leadership. **The theme will be change.**

All markets are transforming today. Most companies are either transforming or need to start transforming in a hurry. **That makes the rule of this age quite simple: lead change or *be* changed.** Getting behind change means losing. Leading change means winning. If you're not transforming the markets you're in, then someone else is doing it, and soon you will be playing by *their* rules. In most markets, it's a rising insurgent brand that's doing the disrupting. ("The Rise of the Insurgent Brand" is another interesting story and an upcoming book from the two of us.)

If the current management, board of directors, or shareholders don't need or want to change from the company's status quo, then they don't need or want a leader like you. And if you value the longevity of your business career, you don't need or want a company like theirs.

The new leadership will be coming of age in global organizations over the next decade. In a few of them, it already has. The new leadership is change leadership.

Today's unprecedented alienation between governments and citizens is caused by the gulf in attitudes toward change. Citizens of the United States and most other countries, like it or not, have gone through fundamental and often catastrophic change since 2009. Government? It just keeps on keeping on. Nothing changes.

Citizens adapt to change, for better or for worse. Governments ignore it, *always* for worse. Citizens are resilient because they must be. Governments are rigid because they can be. Our political research in the United States particularly shows that the citizens—Republican or Democrat, old or young, all ethnicities, all incomes, all levels of education—are ready to rumble. The wild 2016 presidential campaign proves it. In politics, it's called **revolution**. In business, it's called **disruption**.

To lead change today and tomorrow, you are going to have to lead a group, a team, a company, or even a corporation. Gallup does monthly polls measuring "employee engagement." Lately, that engagement number is in the low 30% range. That means about 70% of employees come to work, check Facebook, snooze and doodle through a couple of meetings, play Candy Crush, eat, complain, and go home. Rinse and repeat.

Former Hewlett-Packard CEO and former presidential candidate Carly Fiorina has said the job of leadership is to unlock the potential of your company's people. We agree, but we'd be a little harsher in light of this general engagement funk. We'd say the job of today's leadership is to get those people off their asses and up on the balls of their feet, leaning forward.

The challenge of leadership is to give people compelling reasons to get up and into action.

By the way: "Because I'm the boss" is not a compelling reason. Yes, you can call for action. You can even *demand* action (Dagnabit!). But today's employees, even if they fear for their jobs, will only give *you* a full effort if the full meaning of that effort energizes *them*.

To be a change leader, you have to be a communications leader. You must communicate the meaning of the work and the destination of each project. Studies have shown that communication amounts to more than two-thirds of the leader's job today.

When Ronald Reagan was president, the press often characterized him as "The Great Communicator." They often meant it derisively, their point being that this was all there was to him. His defense came from an unlikely place, *The New Yorker*. It went something like this: "Think about the job of president. He must communicate the complicated workings of our government to the American people. He must gain consensus behind his policies and programs. And he must define America in the world."

As a leader in today's information environment, you have to be a great communicator, period. You can be a genius innovator or a black belt bean counter, but if you can't communicate effectively and compellingly, you're out of luck. If you are going to lead change in your company or your group, you must excite people about the possibilities of change.

We can tell you they won't be excited about the prospects of continual change unless change leads to something important, something great. Change for change's sake is just chaos.

Chaos? It's a situation we've all found ourselves in from time to time, and it's a miserable and untenable situation. Mao Zedong's "Cultural Revolution" was change for change's sake. In rural China alone, historians Roderick MacFarquhar and Michael Schoenhals wrote (*Mao's Last Revolution*), 36 million people were persecuted and between 750,000 and 1.5 million were killed, with about the same number permanently injured. That kind of chaos insulates dictators and oligarchies, at the expense of the good of the people (and, always, always in the *name* of "the people").

Change has to be changing things toward the realization of a positive vision, a New Deal, a New Frontier that leads to a better day for all stakeholders. The two questions leaders of productive change ask are starkly simple: "Where are we going?" and "Why are we going there?" It's your job as leader to answer those questions and define the meaning of the work you and your team are doing together. (In Step 6, you will find a way to answer these questions.)

If you do a 360-scan of the typical corporate cafeteria, it will seem like a mighty tall challenge to get those people moving in any direction other than toward the dessert bar. Can *these* people be turned into winners? Can *they* be turned into an insurgent force that will follow you to victory?

The answer is yes, and history proves it. Others have done it and led their companies to success. Sure, change can make employees in a traditional bureaucracy very uneasy. But it can also make them outperform their potential. Consider that every major corporate turnaround is done with essentially the same people who were failing under an incumbent leader. Under John Akers, IBM was losing relevance, losing market share, and losing faith in itself. In came Lou Gerstner. He not only turned the company and culture around, he did it with the very people who were considered dead weight in the Akers administration. Likewise, in the early 2000s, Mike Roberts led McDonald's out of the deepest rut it had ever been in using the same staff on which his predecessor had blamed his failure. And Bob Iger turned around The Walt Disney Company with the very people in whom Michael Eisner had lost all faith.

By the same token, all the super-smart, super-achiever people in the world cannot overcome a mediocre leader. Almost every tech failure in the past decade proves that.

In politics, the infamous Dukakis for President 1988 campaign team seemed to be the gang that couldn't shoot straight. They were the idiots who put Dukakis in the tank. After a humiliating defeat to Roger Ailes and Bush 41, they skulked away. Yet, contrary to what F. Scott Fitzgerald declared, there *are* second acts in America. That same team, woman for woman/man for man, returned four years later as the "It's the Economy, Stupid!" whiz kids who could do no wrong in running the election of Bill Clinton. The difference between 1988 and 1992? Leadership. Call it "the candidate as CEO." Footnote: Those same people were chosen to run Hillary Clinton's campaign for president. Hmmmm.

So you *can* get them off their asses and on their feet, moving forward. (But it won't be easy.) Employees, just like consumers and voters, are sophisticated, savvy, and very cynical these days. You may expect employee loyalty, but chances are you won't get it for the simple reason that *they* don't expect company loyalty. During the Great Recession, they found that no company was loyal to its employees, not when the BOD, shareholders, and activist investors were screaming for cost cutting.

Do you still want to be a leader? *Why*?

Step 1 is about stepping up. Repeat after us: "I want to be a leader. I want to lead this company or my own company or both. I want to be a change leader."

Okay, we heard you. The next question is *why* do you want to be a leader?

It is important to answer it because that "why" will be the meaning that unites your team behind you. Our friend Fran Tarkenton became a Hall of Fame quarterback not just because of his innate talent and not just because he may be the most competitive person on earth. His HOF career happened because he firmly believed that for *him* to win, *everybody* on his team had to win. For *him* to succeed, *everybody* had to be successful. He went on to lead an expansion team of misfits to three Super Bowls.

So let's turn that philosophy into an audible: "*I* want to win. If *I* am going to win, *you* have to win. So *I* am going to make *you* a winner." Fran has taken that attitude from NFL football into business and made a mega success of the Tarkenton Companies.

A good place to start answering the "Why do I want to lead?" question is at the end. **Think destination:** Where do you want to be when you finish? What will it look like and feel like? How do you want to be seen? How do you want to change the world? What will your obituary say?

We often conduct destination sessions with leaders and company groups to clarify the goals of any project. What is the win? (*More about this in Step 2.*) It's okay to be a little crass and selfish in defining your destination. In a capitalist society, you cannot avoid equating business success with financial success. But Amazon's warehouses are filled with books that will tell you convincingly that financial success is not enough. So, define the effect you want to have on the people around you. How will they think, feel, and behave differently as a result of your leadership? How will *they* define your meaning?

There was a time, maybe in Don *"Mad Men"* Draper's day, when people held business leaders in high esteem. Today, people who are not in leadership positions (for instance, employees, partners, suppliers, shareholders, the press, communities) don't take business leadership very seriously. Are you a CEO? Oh, then you're a *one-percenter*. You're a *suit*. You're out of touch with the 99% or 47% or whatever. In fact, you're an arrogant, egotistical son of a bitch, with your own freaking jet, an exotic set of wheels, and a beach house in the Hamptons, for the love of God! And if you're a woman who leads—well, you're bitchy, you're self-absorbed, you're trying to act like a man, and you are having (they all hope) a miserable home life.

Leaders aren't obliged to disprove these misperceptions. Good thing, too, because there's not enough time in the day/year/century. Nevertheless, they are obliged to recognize them and manage them.

The press will be generally hostile to you, or it will raise you up in the hope of knocking you down again. Be careful. They *really* don't like you. They *really* don't like business. (And that is true of even a good number of so-called business reporters.)

There is an unparalleled alienation from leaders in today's business and political world. There is unprecedented frustration and anger with them. Such is the environment in which you must lead. Welcome to it!

If you want to lead, you must lead for belief, not for the money or the power, and certainly not for the fame and adoration.

Okay, what do you believe?

No matter what you say you believe, employees will learn from what you do, from your behavior—every nuance of it. They'll absorb lessons from all of your actions and interactions. The likes of Gary Hart ("I'm no womanizer ..."), Richard Nixon ("I am not a crook"), Michael Dukakis (Never campaign from the hatch of an M1 Abrams), John Edwards (Oh, behave!), and Mitt Romney (Whatever you say will be heard) taught us that "everything communicates." As a culture, we learn from watching more than from listening. We learn visually. When your words are not aligned with your actions, or when your official declarations don't fit your off-the-cuff remarks, the discontinuity will dilute and finally destroy your credibility.

You will tell the truth, whether you want to or not. That's what we tell politicians at the beginning of any campaign. Likewise, you will tell your employees what you really believe every day in a hundred different ways, no matter what you say. You *will* tell the truth. The best advice we can give you is to tell it fast, tell it all, and, most of all, tell it well.

So it's important to get to the truth of what you believe. It's important to get to the meaning you will represent. People want to work for meaning, not for you. So think it through, very, very carefully.

What is the real meaning of what you do and want to do?
To ask and answer this question was the best advice we ever got,
and it came from Steven Jobs and then from his mortal enemy
Steve Ballmer.

Jobs helped us to develop that model of insurgent strategy
when he asked us to map a campaign plan for Apple vs. IBM and
Microsoft, with Apple as the insurgent and IBM/Microsoft as the
incumbents. To create the model (in partnership with the brilliant pollster and strategist Pat Caddell), we had to decide what
principles the successful insurgents we had worked with used. We
developed both leadership strategies—the insurgent model and
the bigness vs. change model—from that work.

Later, Steve Ballmer asked us to make a speech to the Microsoft
sales force.

"About the political model, right?" we asked.

"Yeah," Steve said. "But make it about insurgent politics.
That's what we want to think like."

"Okay. Like what?"

"Like, do Ten Commandments or whatever."

And we've been doing them ever since. Sure, we've revised and
refreshed the commandments of the insurgent political model,
turning them into highly actionable and absolutely necessary *steps*.
But those original ten were a good place to start. It's a good place
for you to start, too. As you climb through all ten of *our* steps,
think in terms of ten (or eight or a baker's dozen) principles of
business and leadership that *you* believe are immutable for company or personal success. Walk *our* steps, but use them to write *your
own* commandments. Most immediately, please accept the following *seven* commandments to help you chisel out *your* ten (8, 13):

1. ***Start making a daily journal.*** We use classic ruled
   Moleskine notebooks (by the hundreds). Find a pen
   that is not just functional, but fun to use. Write, doodle,

and sketch. Draw connecting lines between fragments of thought. Online, there are several great daily journals. We prefer Evernote, but scout out one that appeals to you and into which you can easily dump interesting stuff from other media, which will recommend relevant reading material and which will allow you to share your notes.

2. ***Write and re-write the ten commandments of your work.*** What principles guide you? We tell politicians that voters are more interested in how you say you decide things than what things you say you will do. They are more interested in the character of your decision process than in the results you promise.

3. ***Pretend you are writing a book.*** Outline your principles as action steps. Begin to borrow from this book and further refine your own strategic framework, the principles and strategies that are at the core, always, of what you do as a business and as a business leader.

4. ***Record who and what in business turns you on,*** really makes the hair stand up on the back of your neck. Read as much as you can about that individual, company, or approach to work. Then write as much as you can about it and what it means to you. As an example, through our work in global politics, we developed a very simple mantra that applies to corporate governance as well: "Democracy is good. More democracy is better. Fluid, highly interactive democracy is best." And we've listed hundreds of examples of highly interactive democratic organizations of all sizes, just as we've listed the autocracies and their outrages. Principle, examples, your experience … on and on.

5. ***Remember to widen your peripheral vision as you chronicle examples.*** Look far beyond the limits of

your company, industry, and sector for examples of the kind of work you want to do and the kind of leader you want to be. Voraciously read and watch and take notes. If it appeals to you, write it down or copy a link to it. Don't worry if it fails to connect immediately to other thoughts. Soon, it will.

6. ***Keep writing and re-writing the principles.*** Keep looking for the bits and pieces of leadership that you want to emulate. The simple discipline of writing and re-writing will not just develop these working principles in your own mind, it will anchor them into your emotions and your physical being—the place where real mastery is achieved.

7. ***Commit to never stop learning.*** Most business people suffer from arrested development: "Everything I needed to know about business, I learned at Harvard Business School ... or my first product manager job at P&G ..." or whatever. Change leaders never stop learning. They look on every meeting, every day, every challenge as another opportunity to learn. If there's one quality common to every great leader we've ever worked with, it is rabid, insatiable curiosity—a hunger for breakthrough. Think of the unquenchable curiosity of Edison, Milken, Disney, or Jobs.

At the same time as you are intently examining yourself and your leadership principles, take a new look at your customers, your markets, and your company. Thinking as a change leader, and thinking in the context of other change leaders you're reading about or listening to, you will see it differently. And keep writing and re-writing your principles of leadership all the time. The ten we did for Steve Ballmer seem a long way back in terms of our understanding of and thinking about insurgent political strategy. We keep learning more about it every day.

Stop Thinking about Yourself for a Minute

Leadership is many things. Your own leadership style and character must be authentic to you. But sometimes the best way to get at that authentic character is to stop looking at yourself and start looking at your customers, your markets, and your company.

Think about your customers first. It's the very rare leader who, through intuition or personal experience, deeply and personally understands the lives, the values, the hopes, and the fears of their customers. More often, we are marketing and selling to people who are not like us. They don't think, act, or quack the way we do.

Sure, we're all data driven today, or claim to be, but in the consulting work we do for our clients, we insist on layering qualitative research—such as in-depth consumer interviews or focus groups—on top of the digital data. Zeroes and 1s simply don't do an adequate job of explaining human behavior. You've got to see it, hear it, and feel it for yourself.

Several years ago when a new version of Microsoft Excel was hitting the market, we forced Steve Ballmer to sit behind the two-way mirror in a focus group room. When it was demoed, this new version of Excel got ooohs and aaahs from Microsoft's product developers and marketers. IT people oooed and aaahed, too—in market research. But *we* talked about it with the actual end users, the people in accounting departments and HR departments in dog food and trucking and aluminum siding companies.

"What's the most important thing about spreadsheet software to you?" we asked.

"The most important? Getting home to dinner on time."

"Having the software get the hell out of my way and letting me do my job."

Honestly, they didn't give a damn that the new Excel could display charts and graphs in vibrant colors, animate them, rotate, and levitate them.

"I don't do spreadsheets. I do my job."

"I'm not in software, I'm in accounting."

Yes, we had to physically restrain Steve from crashing through the two-way mirror a couple of times, but it was great learning for him. He was spending too much time around propeller-heads and not enough around real people. All leaders are to some extent afflicted with separation from the reality of their customers. We like to try to get as "up close and personal" to it as we can.

Learn about your customers by learning their pain points. What pisses them off about your category? What compensations or compromises have they made because of the way your category has developed the user experience? Take canned soda pop. Consumers have never liked soda in cans. They have simply acquiesced to the ubiquity of cans on store shelves and in vending machines. So why do soda pop companies ignore the pissed-off customer factor? It's because cans are easier to stack in the warehouse and on the shelf. It's because aluminum is cheaper than glass. It's because the soda pop companies decided a long time ago, "They'll learn to like it." That was fine when everybody in America was drinking colas and other soda pops, but as they turned to other alternatives, their aversion to cans helped turn them faster and farther from the traditional brands.

Learn the pain points. Steven Jobs was a genius at this. People had to learn the IBM PC's text-based language, MS-DOS, in order to communicate with it. It was a major pain—although Big Blue didn't give a crap. But Steven Jobs did, and along came the Macintosh with its graphical user interface (GUI). No more arcane control key commands. Just click on an icon.

That's not all. Remember when kids had to buy an album of a dozen songs to get the one tune they really wanted? Steven Jobs felt their pain, and Apple birthed the iPod and iTunes.

Who on earth, except for Ansel Adams, ever had a camera handy when they really wanted to snap something terrific? Steven Jobs knew that hurt. Behold the iPhone.

Understanding consumer pain is the fuel of great business leadership. Bill Gates has claimed he never placed any value on marketing. Like Jobs, he said it was all about the product. But, of course, developing a product that implicitly understands people's pain is the best marketing of all. Gates developed the Usability Labs at Microsoft to understand just that pain factor in everyday business and home tasks. How can we make it better? How can we make it easier?

Learn the pain, and you can soon learn to unlock value. Uber founders Garrett Camp and Travis Kalanick recognized that for movers and shakers in big cities, getting a limo meant making a reservation, waiting, and then paying top dollar for the ride. Getting a cab was cheaper, of course, and more conveniently ad hoc—except in rush hours or bad weather. Not to mention that the ride was often uncomfortable, sometimes scary, and left you woozy with strange scents wafting back from the dashboard incense burner. Uber is there, comfortable, and cheaper than a limo. It's a freaking app—a couple of texts. No calling the limo company, and no flagging "Off Duty" cabs in the pouring rain.

Stanley Vergilis co-founded Hux, a promising Atlanta online start-up that provides cleaning services as a product. This is hardly unusual in itself, but Stanley identified the real pain in the marketplace for such services. He understood that cleaning is not the secret sauce that would set his business apart from recommended housekeepers, professional services, and not a few online competitors. His customers are mostly young people, single or recently married, many associated with the tech community in and around Georgia Tech. These Millennials went from not cleaning their dorm rooms to not cleaning their apartments and thus don't exactly have Four Seasons standards. The pain point for these customers is having to deal, personally, with the cleaner. Hux removes that personal interaction. If there's a problem, don't confront the house cleaner. Just text Hux. Even if you want to fire them, text Hux. Hux will take care of it.

When we did some research with Hux customers, all said the same thing. Not: "I love how clean my apartment is!" But: "I love this concept!" Hux is another of those concepts in tech today that are called "The Uber of X." And that's part of the deal in this new economy. A big part of your brand is the meaning of your concept—the *way* you do what you do even more than what you do. Look for the pain in the marketplace. You'll find the value there.

The bigger the pain, the bigger the market disruption. You've been through this situation. Imagine going to a mattress retailer. There are "Sale!" and "One Day Specials!" plastering the windows. A guy who was selling hot tubs last year gives you that big sleazy showroom smile, then invites you to feel like a moron by lying down fully-clothed on several beds for five seconds each. He tells you to ignore the price tag: he's going to give you a BIG deal. Now, you read in *Consumer Reports* or somewhere that if you pay more than 50 percent of that price tag, you're getting hosed. Nevertheless, you are going to feel like you were violated in that purchase experience, and you're going to feel like you need a shower as soon as you walk out. Leesa.com, founded by David Wolfe and Jamie Diamonstein, has been established to be the exact opposite of that experience. We'll talk about Leesa.com more later in the book. It's a memory foam mattress, comparable in quality to the best in the marketplace, but sold only online with just a few clicks at about half the price of the best, delivered in a box and carrying a 100-night no-risk guarantee. That's not just creating disruption, not just a wave; it's creating a tsunami in the mattress business.

Learn how your customers decide. This is particularly important in today's markets, which provide more choice than ever. Determine and probe the context of *their* decision. What we have learned through experience in politics and every kind of business decision, from the most trivial to the most important, is that **people's first imperative in making any decision is gaining a sense of control.** This may be control over their personal security, their family's economic well-being, their health, or their feeling of personal satisfaction. Whatever form it may take, control rules.

✪ More choice means more control for consumers or voters.

✪ Change in the marketplace means more choice and more control.

✪ Customization obviously gives consumers a greater feeling of control, whereas having to lump or like the one-size-fits-all options of the incumbent and obsolescent mass-market marketplace makes them feel like they've lost control—surrendered.

✪ For today's consumers, connection is important, too: connecting to people like them, people they like, and people they'd like to be like.

✪ Oh yes, and in the final analysis, convenience often trumps all other factors.

If you decide to lead, you are going to have to decide to lead consumers to what *they* want. In today's marketplace, the decision to lead is a decision to synch-up *your* decision with insight into *your customers'* decision-making processes.

Learn how your customers decide on re-use or re-purchase. Incumbent businesses cleave to tried-and-true formulas that have been tried and tried but are no longer true. This puts them into direct opposition against today's consumers, who increasingly have the self-confidence to try new ideas. *Free* is, understandably, a powerful concept. But for more and more consumers in today's markets, *new* leaves *free* in the dust.

The size of the early-adopter segment—those consumers who get their social currency from being first to try new ideas and lead others to them—is growing with the growth of consumer confidence in all markets. This means that winning that first trial or first purchase is not nearly as hard as it used to be. Winning that first trial or first purchase is also not nearly as hard as winning the second or third. And, of course, it is only on sustained re-purchase that the cost of acquisition is overcome by profit. Don't kid yourself. Essentially, you *buy* those first "easy" sales. After that, it gets more and more expensive to continue to attract new customers or to attract re-use with price discounts and promotions. Consumer decisions on re-use might be quite different from their decision on trial. Accept this possibility, listen, and learn. Keep your hands on the wheel.

Re-think your market. If you listen hard to your customers, they will undoubtedly make you understand that *they* don't see the market the way *you* do. Deciding to lead requires the courage to decide to be led by your customers' needs and wants.

You may think of your competition as those who line up against you in your category or sub-category. But that's not how your customers see it. Stop fixating on your competitors. Instead, consider share-of-mind, share-of-wallet, share-of-refrigerator, or share-of-stomach. Do so, and your competitive battlefield changes shape. The retailing genius Mickey Drexler, who put Gap on the map and all over the bodies of most young Americans, understood that people who came into his mall-based stores didn't come in to *shop*. They came to *buy*. If they didn't find anything to buy at Gap, they might spend the same dollars not at a competing clothing retailer, but at the Giant Cookie kiosk down the hall. Walking out of the store with nothing wasn't a satisfying experience for the shopper, and Mickey knew it. So he revolutionized merchandising by changing up the selection of looks on an almost daily basis, determined to keep grabbing the attention of his customers all over again every day.

Relevant competition can come from another category altogether. You'll only know what it is if you know your customer really, really well.

Coke and Pepsi created the soft drink market in the United States. Indeed, their competition helped stimulate and grow that market year after year, as it helped stimulate and grow the fast-food industry, convenience retailing, and the motion picture theater businesses. But as times and consumers changed, the big two failed to change their perception of the markets because they failed to see what their customers saw. Worse, as consumers moved to other, healthier, less mass-marketed choices, Pepsi and Coke kept their ICBMs pointed at each other. Now they are being bedeviled not by another giant, but by thousands of insurgent invaders in the soft drink marketplace. It's not the Pepsi Challenge. It's the rise of the insurgent brands. That's the "Real Thing" in the marketplace today. Staring down each other, Coke and Pepsi missed that. And that's why they missed energy drinks, premium teas, juice-infused waters, energy shooters, all-natural sodas, and all of the juice market except orange.

It's all about usage. Increasing usage means increasing loyalty. Of course, you can't get people to buy and use a dud product more often. As advertising sage David Ogilvy observed, "Nothing kills a bad product faster than great advertising." But if the user experience is satisfactory, their usage and ways you can increase their usage—by teaching them new applications, by providing constant upgrades, by intuitive rather than ubiquitous distribution and placement—will help make your customers more loyal and much more profitable customers.

Decide to lead more than the numbers. Markets, it turns out, have some of the qualities of quantum mechanics. Fortunately, you don't need to solve the Schrödinger equation to figure them out. (Schrödinger? Isn't he the kid who plays a toy piano in the *Peanuts* cartoons?)

The bars on a graph of share or consumer purchase behavior may look solid, but they are actually filled with zillions of moving atomic particles, each representing another usage occasion. Forget the bars and focus instead on each usage occasion. They are not all the same. The Mountain Dew a seventeen-year-old landscaper drinks at seven in the morning is a very different usage occasion with a different meaning than the one a thirty-five-year-old insurance salesman picks up at the gas station on the way home from work. *Vive la différence!*

Re-think your company. Don't accept the investor relations definition of your company. Think harder. What is the meaning of your company, the meaning of what you do? What is its meaning *to your various customer groups*—loyalists, first-time customers, those who are not satisfied and give their loyalty to a competitor? What is the meaning to your employees, to your suppliers, to the people in your community?

To decide to lead requires a lot of thinking but even more re-thinking. Here's a helpful exercise for re-thinking the meaning of your company. Go to the beer wall at your local Whole Foods. It is filled with craft brews you've barely ever heard of. They are mostly insurgent brands, and all of them want to take on and beat the big mass beer brands. Write down a few of the names … like Pliny the Younger, Zombie Dust, Focal Banger, or Fat Tire.

Or just do what your kids do when their teacher gives them a research assignment. Google it. Google "20 top craft beers." Now, go to the website of each one of them. You'll find a founder-owner narrative about how and why they decided to start making a special and better beer. Then you'll find a conviction statement—which may be called a "mission" or "vision" statement or, if the insurgent is particularly cheeky, just "What we want to do."

What you will find in checking out twenty or so of these sites is some really interesting ways of looking at the meaning of a little brewery in a big world. All of them (we'll bet you a beer) will have to do with changing the *status quo* ... in the beer business, in their town, or in the world.

Craft beers is an easy example, actually. But you'll find much the same in most start-ups in most industries. All are rallying a small group of young people to sacrifice sleep, pay, and the four basic food groups in service to the success of their little company. This means they will define a greater meaning and a bigger idea they're all reaching for in their work.

No matter the size of your company, the reach of these up-starts can inspire you. It was Leo Burnett, builder of an iconic Chicago-based ad conglomerate, who said, "If you reach for the stars, at least you can't come up with a handful of mud."

Bumper Sticker

Remember those bumper stickers that said "If you can read this, you're too damn close"? Well, if you're reading this, you've not only reached the end of Step 1, you've decided to run for leader.

Prosit! Salud! Mazel tov!

The principles that drive you will continually evolve as you continually learn. The precise moment you actually take leadership may be months or years away. Use the intervening time productively. Decide what you're leading for and what you're leading to. Now, read Step 2.

⭐ Step 2 ⭐
THINK, PLAN, and ACT LIKE AN INSURGENT

Control the controllable. Win the uncontrollable.

Long ago and far away, our original political firm, Sawyer-Miller Group, hired an intern who came to us from Senator Christopher Dodd's D.C. office, Richard Plepler. The kid asked for a meeting with us to say he believed his future would be in business strategy, not politics. At the time, we were doing eighteen to twenty domestic political campaigns a year and dozens of global races. From the perspective of the 1980s, his prediction seemed a hell of a stretch.

Thing is, Richard was a disrupter even then. And he was right.

Fast forward to 2008. Richard Plepler was the new CEO of HBO, which was already riding a wave of success based on its original programming, particularly The Sopranos. *Under Jeff Bewkes,*

41

HBO had fought as an insurgent against broadcast network TV and then-emerging cable movie channels.

By the time Bewkes moved on to become head of all of Time Warner, HBO had become the reigning incumbent of paid TV. And, as usually happens, HBO had begun to think and act like an incumbent. It no longer scouted for new ideas. HBO literally waited for ideas to come to them. By the way, take a number—and don't call us. We'll call you.

Such was the reception screenwriter Matthew Weiner got when he submitted a script about advertising in the 1960s. Mad Men *went on to sweep the Emmy Awards and Golden Globes—not for HBO, but for upstart AMC, which it transformed from a sleepy sort-of-classic movie channel into a paid TV force.*

As shooting for the second season of Mad Men *began in Los Angeles, Plepler, now HBO honcho, did something purely insurgent. He flew to LAX, caught a ride to the* Mad Men *set, talked his way past the security guards, walked in, and got down on his knees in front of Weiner's director's chair.*

"We will never pass on one of your scripts again."

The message was not just for Weiner, of course. It was also for HBO, and it was sufficient to shake the company out of its incumbent culture. Clearly, there was a new sheriff in town, and he brought a saddlebag full of change with him.

Change controls entertainment along with all of today's markets. In fact, every aspect of the current business environment is dominated by change, continual and dramatic. You must prepare your company to survive and thrive in this change environment by creating a change-friendly culture, which is the only way to build an innovation-friendly culture. Ideally, you will teach your people to create the change and disruption in the markets in which you do business. That means you must learn to think, plan, and act like an insurgent, not an incumbent.

Change *is* the status quo now.

Be a Change-Leader, Not a Bigness Leader

In every form of free (or semi-free) election or marketplace, incumbents are fighting an uphill battle. The only advantage they have is superior resources, but, for most, superior resources amounts to so much ballast that slows every move. Everything else leans against the incumbent, including (and most importantly) today's voters, today's consumers, and today's employees. In this age, incumbents slog up a very slippery Everest.

Look around. Insurgent brands and insurgent leaders are on the rise everywhere. They are disrupting every marketplace, every industry, every political campaign, and every part of our society. Yet, amazingly, managers of incumbent organizations continue to tell their people to "act like a leader," by which they mean "act like an incumbent." In this environment, they might as well just say "act like a loser."

Even mega corporations like Time Warner learn to transform culture from incumbent to insurgent. That's the law of survival today.

What's even more amazing is that, in every marketplace, several companies purposely develop their strategy based on that of the incumbent market leader. Following the leader only reinforces the incumbent's advantage, which depends precisely on competitors acting predictably. Unfortunately—for both incumbents and their followers, acting predictably is the very last thing insurgents do.

"Skate to where the puck will be!"

The principles of leadership in long-time incumbent market leaders were written based on past successes. This is not inherently wrong. There is always some useful learning in history. But it must be adapted to the new environment. It must be changed. Or if it cannot be adapted and changed, it must be discarded.

Hockey legend Wayne Gretzky attributed his success to a simple principle that challenged the very first rule of hockey taught to every toddler and junior hockey star: "SKATE TO THE PUCK!" Wayne didn't discard this principle. He changed and adapted it, proclaiming "SKATE TO WHERE THE PUCK WILL BE!"

You want to lead your group or company to where the market will be, not where it is. That's why Steven Jobs disdained consumer research. "The people can't tell you what they want next. You have to show it to them." He was the quintessential insurgent business leader. Although he was written off early in his career as the business equivalent of a juvenile delinquent, he was finally recognized as the revolutionary he truly was. Among those who granted him that belated recognition were CEOs of the companies Apple left in the dust.

Most incumbent leaders are trying to protect the status quo and defend the way the market was—not what it will be. And the one certainty about incumbent leaders today is that they are under attack because the market status quo is under attack, just as the political establishment in Washington is under assault. This forces them to play defense against the insurgent disrupters, who always, always play offense.

Would you rather play defense or offense?

You know the answer, but, still, as we said, in most incumbent organizations, although everyone is hunkered down in a defensive crouch, all hands are told to "act like a leader." Moreover, as we also said, many other companies in the same markets emulate the defensive posture of those incumbent leaders. They want to be the leader, so they think that means acting like the leader, even if the leader is playing prevent defense or focusing only on "not losing."

Think of the NASCAR slipstreaming, or "drafting," tactic, in which one or more cars follow closely in the leader's slipstream so they can ease off the accelerator and save fuel. A lot of companies try to slipstream or draft off of the leaders. Trouble is slipstreaming doesn't translate from racing to business. In fact, in business, slipstreaming has exactly the reverse effect it has in NASCAR racing. In business, drafting fails to pull followers along. It serves only to push the leader farther ahead. At the same time, the more the leader is attacked by insurgents, the more it resists change. The more the leader resists, the farther behind *it* falls—and the slip-streaming followers fall back even farther.

Eventually, they *all* become the prey of rising insurgent companies and brands coming up from behind. And it is their customers who fuel the future growth for the insurgents.

Change and More Change
Are the Only Safe Bets

Change and more change are the only safe bets today and tomorrow. So you'd better be a change leader.

Bob Iger of The Walt Disney Company is universally recognized as one of the top two or three corporate CEO change leaders of the past decade. *Vanity Fair*'s "New Establishment 2015" put him at the top of business leaders in their "Powers That Be" list. But his start on the job in 2005 was almost like some recent SpaceX launches: a very scary disaster.

The incumbent Disney CEO Iger replaced was Michael Eisner. Now, to be fair, Eisner earned a reputation as a genius for taking what had become a very sleepy company, guided as it was by the long-dead hand of Walt, and vigorously building it into a media conglomerate. Like many powerful bigness leaders, however, Eisner became increasingly autocratic. As predictable missteps provoked market and activist investor challenges, he became increasingly insulated, defensive, and more and more and *more* autocratic. And the board of directors? It became increasingly confrontational, giving birth to an insurrection led by investor Stanley Gold and Walt's nephew, Roy Disney. The more they turned up the pressure, the deeper in Eisner dug. Yes, he finally agreed to step down as chairman and CEO, *but* he insisted on naming his own successor.

His choice was Bob Iger, who had been leading ABC television, which Disney had acquired in acquiring Cap Cities Broadcasting. There were plenty of people who thought they saw right through Eisner's crafty choice. Iger was characterized as a charming lightweight, a go-along/get-along manager, who clearly would not object to answering to Eisner as the power behind the throne.

The attack on Iger was immediate and came from almost every side. He was pilloried by the business press, the business pundits, the influencers, the shareholders, and, most of all, by Stanley Gold and Roy Disney.

We had consulted for Bob at ABC, and we liked him a lot. Although we were no longer on retainer with Disney, we e-mailed Bob immediately: "Are you sure you want to take this job? Do you really want to lead this company?"

It was an earnest question. And, yes, it's the same question we're asking you. But, in Bob's case, the sense it made was particularly acute:

A. Bob was already wealthy, healthy, and happily married.

B. He was about to take a job in which practically nobody thought he would or could do well.

C. "B" put "A" at risk.

"If you are sure you want this," we continued, "then you've got to realize that you've been *selected*. To lead, however, you must be *elected*. All of those people who feel you were imposed upon them must be made to feel that *you* were *their* idea. And you've probably only got about nine months to make them feel that way. If you're willing to run *that* campaign, we'll help."

The answer came within minutes of our pressing *Send*. It was, "When can you be in Burbank?"

Working with Bob Iger, we developed a campaign plan to win the votes he needed from voters who, at the moment, saw him as anything but *their* candidate. We started by helping him to develop a stump speech, just as a presidential candidate would. It was important to position Bob as ... well, let's call it what it was: "The Anti-Eisner."

The stump speech was based on a "3x5 card" message we worked closely with Bob to craft. A 3x5 card format is an essential element of campaign strategy, which we will describe for you in detail in Step 6. Suffice to say here that it is the leitmotiv, the earworm you want to plant in the consciousness of those whose support you need to win.

Okay. Throughout his reign, Michael Eisner had communicated implicitly and explicitly to his subjects that nobody really understood the "Disney Magic"—except for him. For this reason, more and more ideas, initiatives, and decisions had to go through him and him alone.

Bob's 3x5 card—title it "The Magic Is Out There"—positioned the quest as "ours," not "mine." It consisted of just six key sentences:

1. Our job is to find the Magic, wherever it is in the world.

2. We must restore our relationship with young families and especially young moms.

3. We must stand for family fun.

4. We must restore our relevance for and relationship with teens.

5. We must be agnostic about how our customers consume our information/entertainment.

6. We must restore the quality of the Disney brand.

It was all "we" and no "I." Hence the Anti-Eisner.

Armed with his 3x5 card, Bob spread his personal version of this six-sentence message through actions and interactions via his direct reports to the rest of the now-sprawling conglomerate. Sometimes, he introduced the first sentence on that card by explicitly disclaiming exclusive ownership of the Disney Magic and that, furthermore, it was nowhere to be found in Burbank, either. It was, he said, "out there," and then he delivered that opening 3x5 sentence:

Our job is to find the Magic, wherever it is in the world.

It's difficult to associate discipline with a man as naturally easygoing and nice as Bob Iger. But he may be the most disciplined leader we've ever worked with in business, politics, or even the military. His actions were as strategic as they were timely. He set about rebuilding all of the bridges his predecessor had burned. He won over Stanley Gold and Roy Disney. He won over the Disney family. He won over Steven Jobs, who had founded Pixar. Even more important, he began winning over the moms and young families, the teens, and more. He allowed the incredibly talented people of The Walt Disney Company to do their jobs, and he never, ever claimed credit for any idea, no matter how successful.

In their revolt against Michael Eisner, the whole Disney organization—shareholders, customers, employees, supplier/partners—had both explicitly and implicitly voted for change. They despaired of getting it in Michael Eisner's anointed, Bob Iger, but Bob Iger campaigned to make their votes for change votes for him. The stakeholders of The Walt Disney Company discovered that they had elected a change leader after all.

Now, let's make sure we're delivering "truth in labeling." We're certainly proud of our work with The Walt Disney Company, but the fact is, Bob Iger is one of the best natural leaders we've ever worked with (and we've worked with Gates, Jobs, Murdoch, Goizueta, Milken, and many others). He's a phenomenal leader who was simply underestimated until he got the CEO job at Disney. We don't want to take any credit for his standout success over ten years at Disney, during which he did nothing less than return the company to the forefront of American family culture. He is a true change leader, as much as Jobs or Gates or Zuckerberg.

Chances are that the people in your markets are voting for change by considering and choosing new options on more and more usage occasions. Chances are that the people in your company are likewise "voting for change" with their arms folded across their chests, waiting for you to inspire them into action. Place the safe bets. Lead for change and more change.

Insurgent Campaign Checklist

We have urged you to develop your own principles of leadership. Through years of work with and study of insurgents, underdogs, and revolutionaries in politics and business, we have developed our own set. Since many of these will quite probably work for you—and you'll see them again and again throughout this book—go ahead and steal some or all of them. Here's the insurgent campaign checklist:

1. Define the Win

✪ Define the metrics of success. Think future state versus present state. What will be the metrics of performance that defines your success? How will all stakeholders think, feel, and behave differently as a result of your success?

✪ Set a "by when" date. Create an "Election Day" for each project and each business objective. Creating a sense of anticipation and a sense of urgency is essential to insurgent success and your success. In politics, every candidate knows what a win is and that it must be achieved by Election Day. In business—not so much. Too often, objectives, goals, and metrics are unclear, vague, or unrealistic. To run a successful campaign in business, the CEO candidate must emulate the political candidate by vividly, compellingly, and unambiguously defining each win *and* each "by when"—each Election Day. In politics, Election Day is a date fixed by law and it's the same for everyone. In business, it's whatever deadline or decision point you set in order to commit the organization to making something happen. If each win must be measurable in absolute terms—get 50.1% or take a hike—each Election Day must be clearly established and absolutely unmovable. In business, Election Days may come every quarter, every month, every day, or many, many times each day. Regardless of frequency, they must be nailed absolutely and without the possibility of excuses.

✪ Define the "win-win" stakes in the election. You've got to communicate how all stakeholders win when you win. Think about how Iger moved the Disney culture from *me* to *we*.

✪ Define the enemy. What's between you and your ultimate win? The eternal enemy is the status quo, and, most often, "us" is a synonym for "status quo." We hear it again and again in company after company: "The real problem is us!"

✪ Define the future. People deserve to know where you are leading them. Iger did it on a 3x5 card, which is usually the most effective way.

2. Do the Doable

✪ Never break your pick on the impossible. Setting unrealistic, unreachable goals will only demoralize your team and energize the opposition.

✪ Remember that you must marshal resources. Don't spend a penny that's not on strategy and pointed toward the ultimate win.

✪ Never meet armies with armies head on. Defeat the competition by flanking them or faking them out of position.

✪ Low-hanging fruit? That's fine, but pick up the fruit on the ground first. Always put the easiest and most obvious goals first.

✪ Get some first downs and gain momentum. Set achievable goals just sufficient to get you moving in the right direction. Celebrate every small victory on the way to the big one. Don't think "Hail Mary" pass, but do get positive yardage on every play. Do whatever it takes to gain momentum in your group and in your marketplace. Play in places where small wins are inevitable. Momentum is magical.

3. Move the Movable

Target only the votes you need to win by defining who is movable and who is not. Spend your time on the former. Ignore the latter.

We at Core Strategy Group look at consumers and employees (and other stakeholders) just as we look at voters: through a prism that makes "attitudinal segmentation" visible as a spectrum. It looks like this:

- ✪ Hard Opposition (HO)
- ✪ Soft Opposition (SO)
- ✪ Undecided
- ✪ Soft Support (SS)
- ✪ Hard Support (HS)

Through this prism, you can look at any group the way we do in campaigns, along a spectrum of attitude. It works to reveal the spectrum of support opportunity of anything from an employee group to a marketplace, no matter how complex or sophisticated the marketplace may be. It is so essential, we think of it as the Operating System of Core Strategy Group.

- ✪ **Hard Opposition (HO):** These people work against you actively. Forget about moving them into positive territory. Fortunately, in most groups and markets, HO represents only about 5–8% of the whole.

- ✪ **Soft Opposition (SO):** They may favor another candidate or brand, but they are not activists. Still, it's too expensive to win them to HS or even SS. They represent about 15–20% of most markets or groups.

- ✪ **Undecided:** Political campaigns will do and spend anything to win the Undecided on Election Day. By Election Day, the Undecided is usually a fairly small, but very important group. You'll do whatever it takes, because you only have to win them over every two, four, or six years. Even the Obama landslide in 2012 was a matter of a few percentage points that were delivered by his campaign's managing the Undecided much better than the GOP did. Obviously, it was worth every cent they spent on winning that crucial group. In markets where purchase decisions—which are "elections" in themselves—happen frequently, daily, or even several times a day, the Undecided votes are very, very expensive to win. Worse, the Undecided are often undecided by character. They refuse loyalty to any one candidate or brand, or their "vote" is strictly determined by immediate circumstances: they are forced to choose on price or location. This means that you can buy their votes with price or promotion, but you cannot buy their loyalty. So you have to keep buying their vote over and over again. That's what we mean by a bad deal.

✪ **Soft Support (SS):** This group might like you or even prefer you, but it won't actively work for you, recommend you, or regularly purchase your brand. Like the SO, they represent about 15–20% of the market.

✪ **Hard Support (HS):** These are your loyalists. They are the solid-rock foundation of success. Though they are a small group (5–8% to begin with), you can turn them into evangelists for you and your brands.

Attitudinal segmentation can be done expensively, with sophisticated data, or cheaply, with guesstimates on the back of a cocktail napkin. You'll find it easy to segment groups you are familiar with, particularly within your company. You choose. Either way, using this system will save you time and make all your efforts more successful. Here are the key plays in our insurgent playbook:

Lock down your HS loyalists, whatever it takes. Nobody but a few saloonkeepers ever went out of business by doing too much for their best customers. Make sure these supporters know your 3x5 card messages, so that they can be as effective as possible in their activism for you.

Move the SS to greater usage and greater loyalty. Use what you learn from the HS to give the SS reasons to like you/your brand better. We find the HS not only knows a brand better from greater usage, they know it differently. That's why we always develop for our clients a "Brand Positioning According to the Hard Support." We want more people to know what HS knows. The same is true for a leadership brand as for a product brand. What do the loyalists know that others should know? Why do they want to follow you? Often, it's not for the reasons you'd expect.

Manage the opposition. Make sure the arguments of the small HO group are not motivating the much larger SO to action against you. You may have to divide and disrupt these two groups when they do unite.

Just forget about the Undecided already. Your life and your money are too short.

4. Build Your Strength Inside-Out

Preach to the choir. Once you've identified your HS loyalists, make sure they know how to work as evangelists for you. Help them communicate effectively with your 3x5 card messaging. Their consistent viral communications reinforce your own messaging.

Transfer ownership of your strategies by allowing key employees and other stakeholders to vet them in early stages of development. Incorporate their (good) thinking. Not only do additional and diverse eyes, minds, and hearts improve a strategy, the contribution gives others an ownership stake, making it *their* strategy as much as yours.

Celebrate every small win. That's what the most successful start-ups do. And, remember, for the people who work for you, recognition is just as important as reward. Create some Heroes of the Revolution.

5. Everything Matters

Remember, two things kill most projects and most rising leaders: lack of focus and lack of a sense of urgency. Become obsessive about details and follow-through. Every one of those details is important in communicating the meaning of what you do and your personal brand. Give your people a sense of urgency by sharing your vision, transferring ownership of your strategies, and giving them a stiff shot of paranoia (What if we *don't*?!). So ...

Remind your people that "everything communicates"—every detail either builds value or subtracts value. No detail is neutral.

Align all of your ideas and tactics behind one core strategy. It is alignment, repetition, and consistency that win campaigns.

Speed wins. But it is discipline, not recklessness, that builds speed.

6. Play Offense!

Never play defense. Use change to regain aggressive control of the dialogue.

There is no value in sameness. Never become a commodity idea. Always look for ways to differentiate yourself and your strategies.

Never take your Hard Support for granted. Focus innovation on HS needs, HS wants, and HS perceptions of pain in the marketplace.

Focusing on the votes you need to win means defining precisely who can make a difference for you. This is an important discipline, not just for efficiency, but also to make your strategic efforts more effective. It also saves you the effort of working for support that won't really make a difference for you. Focus means sharpening everything, every detail, relating to your strategy and tactics.

✪ Step 3 ✪
BUILD Your Kitchen Cabinet

Recruit a core strategy group and build a War Room mentality.

Thirty years after he had invented instant photography and created the phenomenal success of the Polaroid Land Camera, Edwin Land barricaded himself back in the laboratory for his next great invention. He emerged in 1977 with the Next New Thing: instant movie film. (Ta-Dah!)

What Land hadn't noticed while locked away was that JVC's VHS and Sony's Betamax videocassette recorders had already changed the home movie market forever. Movie film? Obsoleted—at least for the amateur. Land's brand-new invention was an instant failure, which cost Polaroid almost $70 million in 1977 dollars—and lost him his job at the company he had founded.

How the hell could that have happened?

CEOs often ask us, "What's the *real* difference between corporate leadership and political leadership?"

In the first place, there are many qualities common to all leaders—more similarities than differences. For instance, *yours* is the final decision, political leader or business leader. In either field, *you* must be the great communicator of meaning and purpose for your constituents, and *you* must focus and energize a huge and sprawling operation.

The difference?

For probably the last ten or so years of a CEO's career, as they rose through senior and executive VP and maybe COO or president, it was never in the best interest of anybody working for them to say, "You're wrong," or "That's a dumb-ass move," or, God forbid, "No!"

If you are a political leader, all you have to do is click through the news channels to hear what a dumb-ass you are. The talking heads will be taking yours off. And even walking the few steps from a comfy limousine to a warm and loving crowd of supporters and campaign contributors in a hotel ballroom, somebody may take a shot at you—possibly even with an actual gun.

It's about insulation from reality. Yes, there are a few CEOs with a truly common touch, who walk the factory floor, cruise the aisles of Walmart to look and listen, or regularly drop into the local non-Starbucks to shoot the breeze. Believe us, they're the minority. Most are insulated by their Mercedes, their corporate jet, the executive john, the secret basement parking space, and on and on.

We all hear a lot of talk about political leaders living in a bubble. It's a myth. The political leaders who live in a bubble are called former political leaders. In a democracy with universal suffrage, no bubble is vote-proof. To be sure, there *are* political leaders whose imperious personalities make them advice-proof. Why didn't any of the dozens of staffers and aides and consultants and paid minions mention to Secretary of State Hillary Clinton that establishing her own private e-mail system was at least sort of illegal, absolutely unseemly, and, in terms of optics, enormously dangerous? The brilliant *Wall Street Journal* editorialist Peggy Noonan had the answer: "She wants what she wants." Nobody at Foggy Bottom or Clinton campaign HQ wanted to risk telling her so and telling her no.

How to Build a Kitchen Cabinet

The president's insulation is far greater, of course, partly due to the obvious need for super security and partly due to the tremendous complexities involved in governing a huge and hugely diverse country. Presidents have polls that describe the mood of the nation from every political angle, and they have advisers to interpret those polls for them. The most successful presidents, however, have always had something else. It's called a kitchen cabinet.

Both the term and the entity date back to 1831 and the administration of that most democratic (small "d") of chief executives, Andrew Jackson. Following a wide-ranging scandal that involved members of his officially appointed cabinet—which the press at the time referred to as "the parlor cabinet"—Jackson began regularly but unofficially and informally meeting with a group of trusted friends and advisors, whom the press dubbed "the kitchen cabinet." President Jackson needed confidants he could absolutely trust to tell him the unfiltered truth, to have feelers out into the Congress as well as the states, and to help him execute on his most important policies.

What Andrew Jackson discovered is that running an organization effectively—actually getting things done—often requires working around the organization itself. This does not mean working alone, but it does mean moving out of the very formal and very public parlor and into the intimacy of the kitchen. As we all know, in any house, the kitchen is where two things happen. It's where all the cooking gets done. And it's where the best, most interesting, and most meaningful conversations take place. (Think of the last party you really enjoyed. Where did you spend most of your time?)

Jack Kennedy essentially reinvented the National Security Council and used it to manage the Cuban Missile Crisis. Yes, that group included the usual suspects—cabinet members and defense and security officials—but Kennedy also made sure that a couple of upstart insurgent thinkers from his administration were in those meetings, which played a major role in determining the fate of humankind.

As a leader in business, you need a kitchen cabinet as much as Jackson and most of the presidents who followed him did. Yes, you've got the board of directors. But how candid can you be with them, especially since three of them sit on the executive compensation committee? You've got your executive committee or office of the president. But how much can you count on *them* to be candid with *you*?

When McDonald's was in its deepest rut in history in the early 2000s—yes, even deeper than its current ditch—when owner/operators were encouraging their kids to find another kind of career rather than handing the business down to them, when Mickey D's was the poster child for junk food, and when tort lawyers were suing the company for making fat kids fatter, it turned to Mike Roberts, one of the most talented lifers in McDonald's management, to turn the situation around.

The company came to the right man, because Mike had a plan, and he called it unambiguously "The Plan to Win." He had developed the plan and had already proven its success in San Diego, then all of California, lifting it from the worst-performing territory in the McDonald's universe to the top-performing. From here, he was promoted to lead the entire West. Applying the Plan to Win here, he won, and that is when McDonald's top management asked him to win throughout the entire United States.

Getting the huge system of the massively incumbent firm together and going on this plan was the same as pushing a steam locomotive with fires banked and wheels rusted to the tracks. He had to make bold moves, and he had to make them fast. This left no time for the traditional consensus building through layer after layer of the bureaucracy ensconced in McDonald's corporate headquarters outside of Chicago in suburban Oak Brook—the remote and mysterious campus disgruntled franchisees (was there any other kind?) liked to call the Puzzle Palace. (It was the very slur U.S. military field commanders slung at the Pentagon. Ouch!)

The thing is, the company that had invented fast food somehow evolved the slowest innovation pipeline seen in American commerce since Henry Ford offered his customers any color car they wanted as long as it was black. So Mike knew he would have to work around the Puzzle Palace to do anything meaningful before taking action and taking it on his own initiative. It was quintessential White House-or-Outhouse leadership. He understood that he did not have to make the detour completely alone. With the essential help of his go-to operations guy, ex-pro soccer player Frank Vizcarra, he created a secret group, his own version of the presidential kitchen cabinet, which he dubbed "The Noodle Team."

The Noodle Team would meet secretly every two months in a nondescript airport hotel near O'Hare. There would be one person from their meat supplier, one from the buns, one from Coke, a couple of veteran owner/operators, two or three field people whose opinion and candor Mike trusted implicitly, his politically trained market researcher Larry Chandler, and a couple of us consultants. Every few months, Frank would cycle in a couple of different players to keep the conversation fresh.

The Noodle Team rules were simple.

✪ Every meeting would be totally unplugged.

✪ Every meeting would be totally confidential.

✪ As soon as Mike walked into the room, took off his coat and tie, and sat down, the truth had to begin: good or bad.

✪ Nothing was off the table.

✪ Agendas were very, very simple:

1. What are we doing wrong?
2. What are we doing right?
3. What are we doing next?

In these meetings Mike forged a *quid pro quo* deal with his best owner/operators: If they brought him an idea they believed in, he'd put it into markets immediately. If he brought them one, they'd do the same. These franchisees were not just top performers, they were also the most credible in the system. So new ideas moved quickly from their markets to the nation and the world. That super-slow pipeline for new ideas was suddenly Teflon coated. The new ideas came gushing out. The Noodle Team meetings were where the revolution began, taking McDonald's from its worst to its best historical performance in less than eighteen months. And for four years, the Noodle Team was a secret to the rest of McDonald's as well as the rest of the world.

For the first year or two, the Noodle Team meetings were brutal. The super-smart, super-cynical market researcher Larry Chandler, who had been trained by Ronald Reagan's pollster Richard Wirthlin, would start with the "What are we doing wrong?" question. The answers came from the mouths (and stomachs) of customers as well as from employees. Ray Kroc had built the chain to honor three key things: quality, service, and cleanliness. McDonald's was now disappointing customers as well as employees on all three. The incumbent culture of the huge company had begun largely to dismiss these three metrics, which had been religion to Kroc. One C-suite executive of the time once wink-winked to us at a cocktail party. "After all, you see, we're not really in the food business. We're in the real estate business."

Oh, well that explained why the burgers were tasting like top soil.

So, we'd limp out of those early Noodle Team meetings and head for the hotel bar. The fact was that none of us then honestly believed McDonald's could ever pull itself out of the ditch. The bureaucracy of mediocrity was too deeply entrenched. But it was Mike Roberts's gritty motto, "Not on *my* watch!" that finally rallied us. It became our rallying cry, our *only* rallying cry. Now that we had control, we weren't going to let this great brand sink like the sun in the dead of winter.

That's why the people in those meetings committed to make the Plan to Win actually win. There was no way this was going to fail—"Not on *my* watch!"

Call it a kitchen cabinet or a Noodle Team or whatever else floats your boat, you need an informal group of people who have the courage always to tell you the truth and always to keep you connected to the reality of the company and marketplace. They may be people in your company, but, very likely, they will be people from outside of it. In most cases, the best move is to combine folks from inside and outside the company, including some industry experts and experts from other disciplines or industries.

Bruce Barlag runs the Global Executive Group (GXG) in Atlanta. It's a terrific service group for leaders and rising leaders in corporations. There are many recruiting firms that specialize in helping a CEO/chairman populate their board of directors with appropriate candidates who will help create a diverse enough group to have credibility with all employees, customers, journalists, and activists. Certainly that's important. What we've found though is that few CEOs/chairmen have the confidence to be completely candid with their BOD. Sure, they have one or two ringers to whom they will go for advice. Even then, though, they don't want to be sweating changes and challenges. And no CEO wants to simply sit back and listen to the board. That seems too passive.

Bruce Barlag puts together advisory boards. These are absolutely not official groups, defined on the corporate org chart. They are unofficial and, like Mike Roberts's Noodle Team, mostly unplugged and off-the-company record. He will assemble groups to help bolster the leader's learning, put some intellectual muscle around a company weakness or market challenge. A good example is the IT advisory boards he puts together. They consist of active or retired IT executives, consultants, or academics. Unlike the official board of directors, they can challenge the leader without threatening the leader. It's about going back to school without the dorm room and beer. The exams are the real business challenges the leader will face day to day. And thanks to Barlag and GXG, the leader can face them with more confidence and a better sense of the options for action.

Whether you're lucky enough to have a Bruce Barlag or Frank Vizcarra to organize and manage the process, you must still have a kitchen cabinet kind of informal learning and advising group. Meetings can be more or less formal. In either case, no minutes should be taken, nothing recorded, no official notes. But the meeting should produce an abundance of commitments to action.

And, oh yes. If you are asking people to be courageous enough to give you a piece of their mind, you'd better be willing to take that piece—whole and without complaint. Snap off somebody's head, and that will be the last time anyone tells you anything except what they know you want to hear. That would be a pity— possibly even a tragedy.

If you decide to get really serious about creating a kitchen cabinet, you can find professional help to optimize the process, include Barlag's Atlanta-based GXG—which, among other things, excels at helping C-suite executives develop external advisory councils to help them become the best leaders they can be. Bruce matches up his clients with other top leaders and subject-matter experts to create an advisory network around his leader-client. He calls it an ecosystem. To us, it looks like a kitchen cabinet on steroids—larger in size and scope than the average kitchen cabinet, but run on the same unfiltered rules designed to save an organization from itself by providing the workarounds leaders need if they are to escape the many narrow silos of incumbent bureaucracy.

Creating a Core Strategy Group

To be dead simple about it, the CEO's job is to make decisions wisely and communicate them effectively. Those two things are tied for first place in importance. To manage that job effectively, we strongly believe in developing a single core corporate strategy that will drive all other division and department strategies. It will be a single communications strategy with which all other communications will align. That makes the CEO's job more manageable and the company more focused.

Most companies we've worked with over the years claim to have multiple strategies going at the same time. Actually, most have multiple tactical campaigns going on at the same time—with no central strategy at all. Strategy is the *why* of an organization or an operation, and tactics are the *how*. Another way to put it is that strategy is the overall plan, and tactics the means by which the plan is implemented. Sun Tzu, the ancient Chinese general and military philosopher, put it this way: "Strategy without tactics is the slowest route to victory. Tactics without strategy is the noise before defeat." In too many companies, that "noise" takes the form of whatever is done that seems to fit the need or solve the problem or calm the crisis of the moment. Sooner or later, however, nothing connects these merely reactive tactical campaigns, and the company veers farther and farther off course—instead of driving a strategy aimed at taking it to the future.

Often, when we bring up the need for a "core strategy," a CEO tells us, "You don't understand how complex the workings of a major corporation are." We respond: "You don't understand how simple they *should* be."

Simplicity in vision, strategy, communications, and action is what makes for focus of meaning, focus on the customer, and focus on the customer's problems. That's why we favor a single core strategy. Developing it is the key to creating a winning campaign in politics, business, or warfare.

Make no mistake, what Mike Tyson said is true: "All plans go out the window the first time you get punched in the nose." Business is done by living human beings, and the essence of life is dynamic. So, yes, you may well need to adapt your core strategy to change. Plans may change and need to change, as General Dwight David Eisenhower learned as his soldiers struggled and improvised at Omaha Beach on D-Day. Even so, looking back, he declared, "planning is invaluable."

It was an understatement. Developing the discipline to unite on one strategy is the key to individual, team, or corporate success. Better have your very best people developing and managing this central strategy. Better empower them to be the *only* people who can change it.

So just who, exactly, should be in your core strategy group?

The well-known, widely accepted Pareto Curve suggests that 20% of the people will do 80% of the work inside any company. In fact, our experience over forty years of working with corporations of all sizes and shapes proves (to us, anyway) that Pareto was mistaken. It's more like 8% to 10% doing 92% of the work. The higher up the corporate ladder you go, the more lopsided those numbers become. In and around the C-suite, fewer people do more of the real, value-producing work.

As leader, your internal Job #1 is to focus on that 8%—which, unremarkably enough, corresponds pretty much exactly to the proportion of Hard Support (HS) loyalists you have. These are the employees most engaged, most focused, and most likely to get the job done. Most likely, their loyalty is not based on blind faith, good buddy-ship, ass kissing (they, yours), or ass kicking (you, theirs). More likely, it's based on a personal need to achieve and shared personal and business values.

You want to nail down this HS loyal group in any way you can, bearing in mind, however, that one size does not fit all in terms of meaningfully managing the most talented people. You also want to develop their skills and sharpen their learning capacity. Help them become the next great generation of leaders. Great leaders are surrounded by great leaders, like Lincoln's "Team of Rivals" cabinet during the American Civil War. Make your loyalists your most effective medium of communications to and through your organization.

The legendary Patty McCord, who was chief talent officer at Netflix for fourteen years, has made a great point about your top and bottom 3%. Her lesson about the top 3% is that the best perk you can give them is more "3%-ers" to work with and have around. She found that all of the formal policies of most HR groups in global corporations are written for the bottom 3%, what we would define as the internal Hard Opposition. Her advice? Don't hire them in the first place. Then you can forget about the rules! Hiring, focusing, and motivating the top 5–8% that we define as the Hard Support is the most important job you'll do as leader.

Your second most important job will be to move the Soft Support (SS), your next-best 15–20%, to more productive and focused work. Where does your core strategy need to be truly brilliant? We think it is in how you manage career paths for your rising leaders. Do not accept off-the-shelf HR training or development programs. Instead, customize career path counseling and development to your company, your culture, and to the individual. Your example and that of your core strategy group will encourage and facilitate continual learning and continual growth. Do anything you can to avoid arrested development of your rising stars. In all ways, your core strategy group will serve as the best communications vehicle you have in your organization.

The so-called core strategy group has traditionally been the strategic hub of any successful political campaign. That's why our consulting company took the name. The core strategy group is the central group of candidate, campaign manager, issue experts, field experts, pollsters, communications specialists, and policy people. It sets the single core strategy that drives the others. It's the big strategic wheel that turns all the others. In political campaigns at the national level, loyalty to one core strategy is assumed as a given. Business, however, has much less a sense of the need to use one core plan as the great strategic wheel that turns all others. You have doubtless found that, in your company, people keep coming up with exceptions to the rule of the core strategy. Most often, this means that they are letting tactics drive strategy. That noise you hear? It's the noise of defeat.

Many corporate leaders we meet with complain that their companies have become "siloed," that each division or department acts as an operation unto itself. The argument the managers of those silos make is always the same: "I'm responsible for the P&L of *my* division/department and I have to be able to do what it takes to deliver on that responsibility."

The problem, of course, is that the silos don't stand separately. Most often, they pull against each other in different directions. At best, your company becomes a holding company that equals the sum of its parts. At worst, it's a drawer full of mismatched socks. The power of alignment is the power of expanding the meaning of your company across all operations and communications, thereby demonstrating that meaning works in many ways but always together. That is true power, which is the reason for creating a company in the first place.

There is another problem with the silos of most large companies. With their separate rules and separate cultures, they look to activist investors on the outside as easily separated, spun off, and sold at a profit for shareholders. They look at the corporation with silos the way a kid looks at a Kit Kat bar: Breaking up is so easy to do!

A core strategy is the glue that holds corporate meaning and purpose together.

Look, all of us in business are temporarily attracted to "shiny objects" in the form of exciting or fun tactics. These days, many are expressed in social media campaigns. That's why we ask our business clients to apply a simple rule of "Strategy Is Boss." This means that all arguments in planning will be settled by answering the simple question, "Is this on strategy?" Nobody can pull rank or play power games if strategy is the boss. Falling in love with a cute tactical approach is fine, as long as it is on strategy. But if it's off strategy, it's out, no matter how adorable.

Corporations today have vision statements, mission statements, purpose statements, aspiration statements, and then an array of silo-based/silo-developed strategies designed to meet specific problems—but which ignore vision, mission, purpose, and aspiration. Contrast this prevailing condition with the simplicity but universality of the famous Johnson & Johnson Credo, a 342-word document written in longhand by Robert Wood Johnson, son of one of the company's founders, over seventy years ago. You can find it on the company's website at the "Our Credo Values" page:

We believe our first responsibility is to the doctors, nurses and patients, to mothers and fathers and all others who use our products and services.

In meeting their needs everything we do must be of high quality.

We must constantly strive to reduce our costs in order to maintain reasonable prices.

Customers' orders must be serviced promptly and accurately. Our suppliers and distributors must have an opportunity to make a fair profit.

We are responsible to our employees, the men and women who work with us throughout the world.

Everyone must be considered as an individual.

We must respect their dignity and recognize their merit.

They must have a sense of security in their jobs.

Compensation must be fair and adequate, and working conditions clean, orderly and safe.

We must be mindful of ways to help our employees fulfill their family responsibilities.

Employees must feel free to make suggestions and complaints.

There must be equal opportunity for employment, development and advancement for those qualified.

We must provide competent management, and their actions must be just and ethical.

We are responsible to the communities in which we live and work and to the world community as well.

We must be good citizens—support good works and charities and bear our fair share of taxes.

We must encourage civic improvements and better health and education.

We must maintain in good order the property we are privileged to use, protecting the environment and natural resources.

Our final responsibility is to our stockholders.

Business must make a sound profit.

We must experiment with new ideas.

Research must be carried on, innovative programs developed and mistakes paid for.

New equipment must be purchased, new facilities provided and new products launched.

Reserves must be created to provide for adverse times.

When we operate according to these principles, the stockholders should realize a fair return.

It is a single-page definition of beliefs and responsibilities, very plainly stated, reminding the company's leaders for all those decades of "our first responsibilities to the doctors, nurses and patients, the mothers and fathers and all who use our products."

We are convinced that a vision statement or a mission statement—one or the other, not both—is a good way to set the sights of your group on the future. It is a destination statement, a statement of where your company is headed; and it is a conviction statement, a statement of what you believe, or your core values and view of the world. But good citizenship and ethical business practices should be assumed, and not necessarily written into your vision statement. For the vast majority of companies today, those are check-the-box "Good Corporate Citizen issues," no different than how many days since the factory had somebody hurt on the job. Vision and inspiration require more than just checking the boxes.

Your core strategy must be simple, yet robust enough to represent the breadth of your business. It is *the* central strategy. In clear language and with impeccable logic, this strategy must define how you will reach your mission as a company. *Mission* is the destination. *Core strategy* is the road map that gets you there.

You should create your core strategy group from among that 8% of most loyal *and* most productive people. If they are loyal without being particularly productive, they are disqualified. The same is true for those who are productive without being particularly loyal.

So your core strategy group must be made up of your most talented people, and not simply chosen by rank in the organization or by job title. You want diversity of background and viewpoint. That's the first requisite for establishing a culture of innovation. And you want to set up a working process that allows for open collaboration. This means that corporate title is checked at the door. You need people who will not be afraid to express their opinions, but who can also listen to the opinions of others. Often, by the bye, this is an exquisitely rare combination. Your core strategy group will be:

- ✪ driven by data;
- ✪ diverse in individuals, backgrounds, approaches;
- ✪ informed by lateral insights—insights coming not just from your brands, customers, markets, and industry, but from outside these as well;
- ✪ committed to open development and open to diverse opinions and approaches;
- ✪ dedicated to aligning all strategies and all communications;

- ✪ committed to the conviction that managing the execution of the core strategy is one of the group's key responsibilities;

- ✪ aware that companies go through cycles of centralization vs. decentralization and therefore committed to centralized strategy and decentralized execution;

- ✪ willing to bring trusted insights from the field when possible;

- ✪ willing to face change;

- ✪ biased to create change in your markets;

- ✪ capable of developing scenarios of possible marketplace changes and hypotheses of new actions to meet challenges and seize opportunities; and

- ✪ willing to set a *by-when* date for any project or plan, because without an Election Day defined there is less urgency and focus on a given project or plan.

Your core strategy group sessions, like Mike Roberts's Noodle Team sessions at McDonald's, must be unplugged. If your people are afraid to tell you the bad news, you'll find that bad news creeping closer and closer to your campfire—as Hillary Clinton found in 2007–2008. These sessions must be respectful, but frank and honest. As always, you will set the tone for the respectful, candid, and open environment. Don't just listen to the outlier opinions: *hear* them.

Within the core strategy group, you need a quarterback to help drive the sessions and monitor actions coming out of them. At McDonald's, that was the very talented Frank Vizcarra. He served the requisite triple role of quarterback, coach, and referee.

Some individuals will rise to the top of an organization on their own talent and energy. But sustained and successful leadership depends on building a solid team. That team, your core strategy group, will be the engine of transformation for the entire organization. As a reflection of your leadership, the core strategy group will be the central driving force in development of your company culture. Change leadership must eventually engage an entire company and the company's system. Bob Iger, The Walt Disney Company CEO, helped us develop a definition of a strong culture. In it, every employee can say three things:

1. "I am a part of something great."
2. "My individual effort can make a difference."
3. "Somebody recognizes my difference."

Driving cultural change into every corner of your organization and system starts in the corner office. *You* must be willing to change your own approach, so that you are more open, more inclusive, and invariably, fundamentally truthful. Fail to change in order to achieve these three things, and you will become isolated from the reality of the marketplace, the reality of your corporate culture, and the reality of a world where people call a dumb idea a dumb idea.

✪ Step 4 ✪
PREPARE Your Campaign Inside-Out

Understand the power of brand. Create a winning project.
Use the power of inside-out communications.

Revolutions are built inside-out. They begin with one charismatic, idealistic, and committed leader, who is joined first by a cadre of close disciples who together foster a growing crowd of loyal supporters, who give rise to a cascade of followers until the revolution becomes an unstoppable force.

The power of the revolutionary idea builds inside-out. Like everyone else, we've heard the admonition "Don't preach to the choir," but, as students of and advisers to several revolutionary movements, we know better. Successful revolutions focus first on the "choir," that small band of fervent believers. Successful

75

revolutionary leaders preach to them first, turning them into missionaries and evangelists to spread the gospel of their revolutionary idea.

This is the way each of the world's most powerful religions began—all that are more today than footnotes in historical encyclopedias of religion or, worse, dictionaries of mythology. And it is the same in politics or business. We told you that you cannot get to leadership—or succeed in it once you reach it—on your own. Think we're making this stuff up? It's history. It's civilization. It's Julius Caesar, Elizabeth I, Napoleon, Jesus Christ, Muhammad, Mohandas Gandhi, Steven Jobs, Ted Turner, Corazon Aquino, and, oh yes, the founding fathers of the United States of America. All have one thing in common: They built a compelling following.

By contrast—revolutionary leaders who do *not* build a following? They're around, too. They are the people you see wearing caps of aluminum foil and muttering to themselves on a park bench surrounded by a loyal legion of pigeons.

You need the capability of building support for your ideas and, yes, for you, personally, as a leader. To develop this capability, you will need mentors who become your Kitchen Cabinet and a core strategy group—to help push forward your leadership ideas. Working with them, you will need to win more and more Hard Support (HS) loyalists and, in due course, add to them the Soft Support (SS) from whom your HS cadres are replenished and expanded. By then, you've got the revolution that cannot only sweep you into leadership, but also bring your company or team along with you.

The Brand of You

In this step, we tell you how to build strength inside-out, starting with you. It's a given: Every political campaign begins with the candidate. That's you. In today's terms, your viability as a candidate is expressed in terms of the meaning and strength of your personal brand. Naturally, the title and job description of CEO tends to certify your brand, thereby adding to its meaning. Your personal leadership brand, however, must be established a long time before the letters C, E, and O are added to it.

Think about political figures globally and how easy it is to define the most familiar brands: Washington, "The Father of His Country"; Lincoln, "The Great Emancipator"; Reagan, "The Great Communicator"; Margaret Thatcher, "The Iron Lady." Then there are the presidents whose brands come down to a set of initials that bring to mind a whole set of qualities: TR, FDR, JFK, LBJ. And names like Putin, Obama, Kim Jong-un, Trump, and Hillary trigger emotions, positive and otherwise, the way Pavlov made dogs salivate at the mere idea of a meal.

Now narrow your aperture to focus on your own company. Think of any five people you know well there. How would you describe them in three to five words? Savor those words, the good and the bad. Sweet? Sour? Appetizing? Disgusting? Or just plain bland? Take a moment to clear your palate, then read this sentence: What you have just done with them, they can do the same with you.

And they do. They do it every day, before, during, and after every interaction they have with you.

So now you know why it's so important for you to vigilantly manage the meaning of your own brand. **You must control the dialogue about yourself among all stakeholders. You must be your own brand manager—because if you don't manage your own brand, your competition will be happy to do this for you, or, almost as bad, that definition can be left to the whims of the information age. Never forget this.**

We've already admitted it several times in this book: We have often been accused of telling *political candidates* they need to think in terms of *brand marketing* and telling *corporate leaders* they need to think in terms of a *political campaign*. Guilty as charged.

Business leaders are naturally more accepting of the notion of branding than political leaders, but both are often a little uncomfortable when it comes to branding themselves. Brand? A brand is what Snickers has, not the CEO of Mars, which makes that candy bar—and not a United States Senator, who eats it.

Right? Wrong. Dead-as-a-doornail wrong.

We are not anthropologists or psychologists or epistemologists, so we cannot tell you with any empirical authority that human beings are hardwired to see the world in terms of brands. We are not theologians, so we cannot tell you that religion involves divinely inspired branding. We do, however, understand contemporary culture pretty well, and it is crystal clear to us that, in our culture, all things are understood in the way that brands are.

Asking what came first, the cultural impulse to brand or the influence of commercial branding on culture, is a futile question. Just accept the fact that branding is the fastest and most compelling way to attach a handle on something or someone, and, at this point in the Second Millennium, branding has been so thoroughly developed in marketing practice that we have all been learning marketing all our lives, like it or not. The accelerating technology of mass broadcast communication and its even faster eclipse by interactive digital communication have added urgency—welcome or not—to our lessons. Put it this way: In an age of 140-character messaging, the shorthand of brand communication, always extremely useful, has become absolutely essential.

Problem/Solution

As with the product brand, the context of the personal brand comes from marketing. We all swim in marketing messages up to our snorkels 24x7x365. Marketing has made a science and art of quick, compelling communication, of packaging, and of labeling. Marketing decisions—buy/don't buy ... don't do it/just do it—run throughout our days with the relentless persistence of the beat, beat, beat of the tom-toms. Even complex decisions tend to be framed in the context of consumer marketing. The most common such template is "problem/solution."

Problem: "Hungry, but don't want a meal?"

Solution: "Have a Snickers!"

Consciously or not, consumers use this template not only for making casual purchase decisions in which the stakes are under a dollar but over 200 calories. They also, for example, use this template in technical and industrial categories, where purchase decisions may run into the millions of dollars.

And consumers of political leadership?

Courageous, tough, and credible on defense, but compassionate and a little nutty—much like a Snickers bar: John McCain.

So, get over it. You are a brand.

The Problem of *But*

You are a brand. Okay, yes. Admittedly, you are more than that, of course. But you are also that. You will have a brand, and you will begin to develop it long before you are running for the office of CEO. How do we know this? Because it happens to everybody who wasn't sentenced to solitary confinement back in toddlerhood. You—everybody—will have a brand, whether you develop it or not. The thing is, just as it's very risky to accept the default password that comes with an online account, it's even more dangerous to accept the default brand others may shape for you—especially if they don't particularly like you. One of the lessons you'll learn in Step 6 is to define yourself before your opponents do the job for you. And again, make no mistake, they will always be very happy to do that job. If you are defined even by friendly competitors, your brand positioning—your personal brand relative to the personal brands of others in your company—will almost always include the word *but*. To wit:

"She's very smart … but … a little bit of a bitch."

"He's my go-to guy … but … he just doesn't get the best out of his team."

It gets to the point that you naturally wait for the *but* when you hear or overhear anyone described in the break room or in the course of after-work cocktail conversation. You *know* this is true, so take some time, right now, to examine your own *but*, as it were. What do you think it is? You may not have to guess. Frequently, the *but* will appear in performance reviews over the years: "He really knows this category … but … he's just not proactive in taking on the category challenges."

So, don't wallow … but do own up. Ask a good friend or two at work to frankly address any inconsistencies in your brand. An "inconsistency" is the "but" in your performance.

"Snickers is a great, satisfying snack … but … it's about 98% sugar."

"No doubt Barack Obama is a smart man … but … he's not a real leader."

Inconsistency dilutes any product and can destroy it, whether the brand is corporate or political. Remember John Edwards? "Great haircut, and he sure does care about the poor and oppressed … but … he cheats on his dying wife."

You don't need to be saddled with John Edwards–size inconsistency to cause damage to your personal brand. Among today's savvy and cynical audiences, a product that doesn't live up to its own brand promise is dismissed in a split second, and the bad brand experience of a few will be broadcast by word of mouth as well as by word of mouth amplified and ramified via social media. This goes for a bad product experience or a bad work experience.

In building your brand, identify the *buts* and devise ways to replace them with *ands*: "She's very smart ... and ... she's great at organizing a project team."

Everything Communicates

Brand failures from the world of politics—think John Edwards or Gary Hart or Mitt ("47 percent") Romney—leave behind valuable scar tissue in the form of a lesson that can be stated in a single noun and a single verb: **Everything communicates.**

Every detail is important in forming your brand.

Think about the experience of choosing a product on a shelf. All other things being equal—your significant other has not sent you to the store specifically to buy Brand X—you are influenced by the tiniest details that connote (for instance) quality, freshness, or natural ingredients positively. Or, negatively, they communicate the opposite. Those products that are heavily negative don't stick around too long, but even those that present some mix of positive and negative messages fail to get chosen. The clarity and consistency of positive brand messaging wins. Transpose this maxim to the task of analyzing and developing your personal brand. Get beyond the broad strokes and the vague values. Think about your brand in terms of the details.

But we're getting a little ahead of ourselves. Remember that the first step in the classic recipe for rabbit stew is *First, catch your rabbit*. **The *first* rule of building a strong personal brand is the same as building a strong product brand: First, create a terrific product.**

Before you work on your brand as an expression of who you are, work on who you are. In addition to studying your annual performance reviews, which may be sugarcoated, seek out the frank assessment of mentors and of those in your organization you trust, people who may not even have direct authority over you. If you are rising in an organization, think hard about how your personal goals/values align with corporate goals/values or the goals/values of the current leadership. How does your performance support these goals/values? How can you play more effectively to your strengths? How can you shore up weaknesses and fix problems?

Building Your Brand

Your intelligence, talent, and initiative will come through in your actions. So, too, will the interpersonal skills and communication skills required of a leader. Nothing communicates brand value like the product quality and product experience. Our actions and interactions tell the truth, whether we want to or not.

Far too many market-leading companies are too slow to improve their products as a way of improving brand value. It's only when they are challenged by an insurgent that they look to make meaningful changes. Just check out the shelves of your supermarket today. You'll see the old standard brands with new standards of "improvements" introduced to be more natural, more sustainable, and more appealing to new and more exotic tastes. And the most important thing you can do for your personal brand is to improve your product in real, not "incremental," ways—and then keep on improving it, continually revisiting, revising, and refreshing what you do and how you do it.

Real improvement also happens to be the most important thing your company can do to enhance its corporate brand. This includes improving the quality of its leaders, managers, and employees. We got into the training and coaching business because the level of quality in off-the-shelf status quo training programs is that of mass-market beer before the craft brews appeared. In fact, we believe that **"craft training" is the next new thing**. The value of no corporate asset can be improved as surely and affordably as the quality, initiative, and agility of your company's people. So, short of personal coaching from Core Strategy Group, think of the ways you can improve your own personal "product":

✪ There is always more to learn about your company's products, your customers, your markets, and your industry's competitive map.

✪ You can take advanced courses in areas of business that may lie outside of your greatest strength or focus but that are nevertheless important to the company. Finance is an area too important to be left exclusively to the CFO, and the CFO really should learn more about marketing as a process to add value to transactions. Decidedly, marketing is too important to be left to the marketers.

✪ You can stimulate your ability to learn by exploring personal pursuits like art or history in parallel to your work. You'll find the cross-pollination is positive. The best leaders we've worked with are constantly finding useful context and parallel learning in lateral subjects that are apparently remote from business.

✪ You can improve your interpersonal and communications skills—by reading this very book, for instance.

✪ You can improve your appearance, energy level, concentration, and physical as well as intellectual stamina by devoting yourself to fitness. A training discipline, whether triathlon, yoga, or Tae Kwan Do, is as important as any other leadership discipline.

Enhancing your skills and your performance are the first places to start. Next, consider how the components of your personal brand will be developed. Truth to tell, it's the same for you as for "New Tide HE Turbo Clean Plus Downy April Fresh Scent." Tide's a brand. You're a brand. The components of all brands—product, organization, individual—are the same:

1. Presence/Awareness
2. Relevance
3. Differentiation
4. Credibility
5. Imagery

1. Presence/Awareness: "What's-her-name seemed to have a lot of great questions in that meeting today." Yep, building brand value begins with building brand awareness. You've got to *be there*, and they've got to know who you are.

Marketers worship at the altar of simplicity. Above all else, they keep it simple. Go thou and do likewise. Never identify yourself with your full and formal name. Compress "Elizabeth Rowlands Smith" to "Liz" and "William David Smith, Jr." to "Bill." In all but the most hidebound and history-encrusted institutions, formality confers no power today. Even the Sovereign Military Hospitaller Order of Saint John of Jerusalem of Rhodes and of Malta just calls itself the Knights of Malta these days, and the chairman and CEO of one of the most powerful and respected corporations in the world is known throughout the campus of Johnson & Johnson and in the 60 countries where J&J does business as Alex. Think "Anheuser-Busch's Budweiser" vs. "Bud." Which is the better call in a bar on game night?

Make it informal and you make yourself accessible. As a leader, the last thing you want is a barrier between you and your people or you and the reality of your organization and your customers. Talk, write, and sign in the same simple, informal, clear, and respectful way. Make a point of using e-mail or text in congratulating, encouraging, or empathizing with the people in your group.

Making it simple is the simplest way to get your name out there. *Keeping* it out there requires that you also step up to the jobs others may not want to do. Don't grandstand, and don't kiss ass. "Liz the Showboat" and "Bill the Ass Kisser" are really terrible personal brands. And do keep your name out front by associating it with solving problems at work: "Liz the Problem Solver." "Bill the Go-To-Guy." In product branding, acceptability begins with availability. In personal branding, they've got to know who you are to begin to consider you for leadership. Get your name in the game. Keep it there.

2. Relevance: Every successful brand provides benefits that are relevant to its target audiences. Unsurprisingly, marketers call these "relevant benefits." The brand has to solve problems, remove pain, fulfill desires, help realize aspirations. The more personal the relevance for any consumer or consumer group, the better. Political promises are always aimed at pain in the electorate, whether it's "the economy, stupid," "our broken immigration system," "high prices," or simply a more generalized frustration with the status quo established, maintained, and represented by "the political elite," namely incumbents of both parties, lobbyists, big business, big unions, big banks, big special interests, and big media.

For four decades of presidential elections, Americans have consistently voted for change, but seldom got the change they voted for.

Incumbent politicians will list their accomplishments in terms of problems solved for their constituents. And since so few incumbents in Congress actually solve problems these days, they'll list the issues they "fought for." That's Congressional code language for going to a couple of committee meetings and reading prepared statements. Insurgents make promises about how they will solve those problems *differently*. How do you create relevance for "the brand of you" in business?

✪ Be a "problem/solution" brand. Use your journal to
   outline any project or duty in terms of the simple prob-
   lem/solution framework.

- ✪ Define the problem. Make sure you've defined it clearly and completely. Too often projects are focused on solving the *wrong* problem. In coming up with your definition, think 360 degrees around the issue at hand.

- ✪ If it's a problem of weak demand, make sure to pore over the market research. Read the verbatim responses and watch the video of qualitative research focus groups or in-depth interviews. As psychoanalysts tell their impatient patients, understanding the problem is the only way to a lasting solution.

In our work, we use a concept from psychology, pattern recognition, to clarify the process of defining the problem. For us, pattern recognition is the "aha moment" in an analysis when you can begin to relate and assemble different pieces of data into a recognizable form. With years of corporate and political experience behind us, we often note this moment of recognition with the same remark: "We've seen this movie before."

Early in the process of defining the problem, even at the stage of using single words or simple phrases, begin jotting down possible solutions. Start with the most obvious: If there's a hole in the bucket, plug the hole. In defining the obvious solution, don't necessarily let "practicality" rule out hypothesis development. If the answer is too expensive, takes too long, or involves a partner who "would never go for that" or some other normally game-ending obstacle, don't dismiss it out of hand. Years ago, while working with Castrol Motor Oil, we were briefed by the company's technical experts. They told us, in so many words, that all motor oils are exactly the same, and even the 10W-20 vs. 10W-30 vs. 10W-40 is a meaningless differentiation.

"Hey, isn't there *something* that could be done to make your motor oil better and different?" we asked in some exasperation.

"Well," one of the engineers drawled, "these little four-banger engines today burn mighty hot. A little more viscosity would be a good thing."

"So ... could you do that?" we kept on pushing.

"Oh, that would be really, really expensive."

He meant to dismiss the idea.

"*How* expensive?"

"Oh, maybe a two- or three-hundred-thousand-dollar change to the process," he said without an ounce of irony.

With the enthusiastic permission of their late, great CEO, Martin J. Donahue, the changes were made, and Castrol began a thirty-year roll with "The First Oil Engineered for Smaller Cars."

As you develop potential solutions into more formal hypotheses, draw lines to key points in the company's objectives and strategies—literally: actually draw the lines. You will begin to see which points in your hypothesis are in direct alignment with your company's overall business objectives and which lines lead elsewhere. Draw circles around those solutions that are in line (literally, actually) with company objectives and strategies.

Everything you do in your company should build value or add value to transactions and add enduring value to your product brands and corporate brand. Too often, projects are about "working on" a problem or "addressing" a challenge. That's not good enough to provide true relevance. Evaluate each initiative or project as problem/solution opportunities. It should work like this:

- ✪ Find the solution.
- ✪ Solve the problem.
- ✪ Eliminate the pain.
- ✪ Create new value.

Work it this way, and you'll know you are providing relevant benefits that endow your individual, product, and corporate brands with relevance.

3. Differentiation: The simple fact of all markets is that value is created by scarcity, not sameness. Relevant differentiation—solving a marketplace problem in a unique way—is the key to the enduring value of Starbucks, Google, Porsche, and Samuel Adams. It can be for you, too. Being the same as the top five people in your position is not good enough. In fact, it stinks.

The truth is, if you actually solve problems instead of kicking them down the road a few yards, you'll not only create relevant benefits within your organization, you'll differentiate yourself.

Focusing on the solution is key. And defining the "by when" is a relevant differentiator. Individually, be the one who helps develop a sense of urgency, and not panic, in your work and at work.

While the capability of urgently focusing on solutions is a key differentiator of your personal brand, so are other aspects of your performance, work process, background, experience, and personal style. Play to your outstanding strengths, but never forget that differentiation without relevance is just flamboyance. Make sure each of your differences is associated with relevant benefits. As we say to product marketers, make sure your difference makes a difference.

A final word about differentiation. It's not all about talking or even about doing. In today's high-speed workplace, *listening* has become a compelling differentiator of your personal brand. Most people don't take the time to *hear* what others are saying. Or they selectively hear only what they themselves have said in the meeting.

In a continual but ever-fruitless back-and-forth with a spouse over who was mumbling and who needed a hearing aid, one of your authors decided to have his hearing tested—less for potentially therapeutic purposes than to settle the argument.

"The doc says my hearing is perfect!" he proclaimed.

"Then you're hard of *listening*!" she replied.

Don't just hear. *Listen.* Prove you are listening by acknowledging and responding. A no brainer? On the contrary, a big brainer—for the simple reason that listening is increasingly scarce these days at the kitchen table or the workplace. Scarcity = relevant differentiation = value. Besides, you might actually learn something.

4. Credibility: Your credibility is the bedrock foundation of your personal brand, especially when you work on a team or in a company. Credibility is the sum of the promises you make subtracted from the results you deliver. Promise more than you deliver = low credibility. Deliver more than you promise = high credibility. It's that simple. It's that hard.

The bar marking the threshold of credibility is higher these days because of popular cynicism resulting from decades of dominance by a political elite that constantly over-promises and under-delivers and a marketing class that over-hypes products that under-perform. Is it any wonder that cynicism runs high?

Working for client Microsoft in search of a successful model of customer satisfaction, we focused on Southwest Airlines, long the customer satisfaction leader in the airline category and, in fact, the leader in customer satisfaction across many other categories as well. The formula we came up with works for building product, team, or individual credibility. (If only the political class would use it!) Here it is:

$$D + O + C = S$$

D is **Define expectations in advance**. Unambiguously define what you intend to accomplish with a task, project, or, as the case may be, your CEO leadership platform. Clarity—the absence of ambiguity—is essential to focusing yourself, your team, and all those who will judge your results, namely all stakeholders. If expectations are not clearly defined in advance, others will not judge *your* work on *your* terms. Controlling the dialogue about you and your leadership is an imperative of successful leadership. So it's back to defining the problem clearly and then defining the solution in the same clear terms.

As a corporate leader, you may be facing more than a few challenges, each of which requires a different solution. The same strategic framework applies, challenge by challenge.

In communicating your proposed solution, follow the Southwest paradigm by setting expectations modestly. Unlike its competitors, Southwest Airlines doesn't provide reserved seats, first-class, or upgrades. The airline doesn't even attempt edible meals or fine wines. What they do, however, is promise a terrific service attitude without any of the bullshit fees and boarding-gate battles that drag down the other major airlines. Follow this leader by making sure you don't over-promise the solution you recommend. Keep it simple. Keep it modest.

O is **Over-deliver on a highly relevant attribute**. In the case of Southwest, it's that unmatched service attitude, which is constantly contrasted with the competitive big three airlines: Delta, American, and United.

The comparison seems almost unfair. Burdened by their promises, the other airlines are busy arguing with passengers over upgrades, changing seat assignments, or assessing baggage fees. Southwest focuses its passengers on just one relevant factor—service attitude—which just happens to be the one in which the airline is unquestionably superior to the rest.

True, early in its corporate life, Southwest developed a reputation for cheap fares to business destinations. Southwest's fares are no longer cheap, let alone the cheapest, but they still look good relative to the big three, especially when seen in the glaring, migraine-inducing bare-bulb light of the big three's strategy of grafting add-on costs to what should be included services.

Over-deliver on the solution *you* recommend. And remember, it's easier to over-deliver when *you* have set the bar of expectations as low as possible.

C is **Claim your success with key stakeholders**. Remind them of how you over-delivered on the expectations you yourself set at the beginning of the task, project, or initiative. Don't boast. Just record the facts. Put it in writing. Leave a paper—okay, digital—trail that will enable you to communicate the metrics of success. With luck, the numbers won't add up. They will exceed, demonstrating in dollars made or dollars saved or units produced or satisfaction created that you have exceeded your promise by over-delivering on goals. (Goals you have set, mind you.)

Clearly communicate how key targets of your task/project/initiative think, feel, and behave differently as a result of your success. Be sure to define "success" in terms of (your) "goals." Always, control the definition of success. Never leave it to others.

S is **customer Satisfaction**. In the case of building a positive personal brand, this means satisfying any and all who will judge the results of your work.

This gets us into the area marketers call **brand imagery**. In a personal brand especially, credibility needs to be an important part of this imagery. Nevertheless, your brand image must be based on solid performance and an unambiguous approach to communicating about it.

All brands are associated with some imagery, whether the brand is for a product, service, company, organization, political party, political candidate, CEO, or other individual.

With product and service brands, customer usage experience trumps—and shapes—all other forms of imagery.

No fancy packaging or funny advertisement can overcome an unhappy usage experience. You can add packaging to the experience with your brand in terms of appearance, fashion sense, humor, or "plays well with others." But the package must amplify a positive "usage experience." In the case of a personal brand, usage experience is determined by your actions and your performance as well as the overall experience of working with and for you. This is the truest imagery of a leader.

It isn't a louder voice or sharper pants suit. It all starts (or stops) with performance. The high visibility of the political stage in the United States and most other countries has put on display the full spectrum of buffoonery in leadership imagery as imagined by ersatz leaders. Puffery, faux power symbols, and bad haircuts infect the political class. So we all have plenty of practice in identifying the leading indicators of self-inflated and self-declared leaders. Bankers wear banker costumes. Engineers wear short-sleeved dress shirts. And, boy, are we bored with the CEO imagery of the tech start-up. Jeans and cargo shorts signify distance from the grown-up business world. A profusion of toys all over the office connote creative thinking, as do the natural foods growing mold in the breakroom fridge.

These days, thanks to the pervasive influence of marketing in almost all cultures, we are all jaded critics of the theater of leadership. Our bullshit meters are super-sensitive, set on hair triggers all the time. So beware.

Remember the "Power Tie?" Well, forget the Power Tie. The point is that the power is behind the tie. The most effective imagery puts your actions out front. Support what you do with a no-nonsense look that says you want to be judged on your function, not your fashion.

Branding the Company

As a business leader and the leader of a business, you need to brand your company in ways that amplify even as they are amplified by your personal brand. The problem is that when most corporate leaders think "brand," they think first and foremost of the superficial aspects of imagery, including the logo.

Predictably, much of this thinking occurs when a corporation faces a crisis with a tide of negative imagery, leaders call in designers and consultants to redesign the logo and come up with a new name; they will change that logo, or even change the name, as Philip Morris became Altria, Comcast became Xfinity, and Blackwater, the private military contractor that become famous for all the wrong reasons during the Iraq War, became Xe in February 2009 and then Academi in December 2011, a reference to the Academy of Plato and a name chosen, according to the firm's CEO at the time, Ted Wright, to deliberately convey a more "boring" image.

In his posthumously published unfinished final novel, *The Last Tycoon,* F. Scott Fitzgerald proclaimed, "There are no second acts in American lives." Although that was pretty much the case for F. Scott, Americans have a seemingly limitless capacity for handing out second chances. America has long been a land of inventors, true enough. Even more true, America is the land of re-inventors, and our people welcome re-invention and grant a second chance … provided that—

- ✪ There is an acceptance of responsibility for the consequences of the first chance.

- ✪ There is sincere contrition. (Up until the Takata fiasco—airbags that explode with the force of pipe bombs—Japanese business leaders were doing this very well.)

- ✪ There is a clear effort to change.

Fail to meet these three conditions, no two-million-dollar logo makeover will turn the opinion of cynical stakeholders. Xfinity has been a success in changing the public dialogue about Comcast, which had one of the worst customer satisfaction reputations since Nero played with fire. The name change was a good idea, but it was presented as a new label for a new approach to doing business, which included a thorough redo of customer service and customer relationship attitudes. Without this basic product redesign, a new name and a new logo won't do a thing. Corporate sleight of hand doesn't work for long in a transparent-information environment.

So, every corporation has a logo, but only some of them have a brand that is consistent with it. Think of John Deere. Founded in 1837, the company has a timeless yellow-and-green leaping deer logo and a tagline to match ("Nothing runs like a deer") and—oh, yes—it produces products with a high consistency of performance and value that harmonize with the logo and tagline. This concurrence of brand imagery and brand substance is what makes successful and durable brands. At its best, this represents a near perfect alignment of imagery and performance—and the CEOs who run this best have personal brands that, at the very least, introduce no dissonance into the sweet music.

The two principal components of any corporate brand are—

what it does + how it does it

Over time, this becomes—

what it does + how it does it = corporate reputation

Our work with and research for our clients have taught us that corporate reputation is a palpable and powerful fact. A corporation's reputation affects

✪ every transaction,
✪ every relationship,

✪ every communication, and

✪ every interaction.

This means that it impacts

✪ the market value of its brands,

✪ supply chain and demand chain efficiency and effect,

✪ recruiting and retention of talent,

✪ shareholder and analyst attitudes, and

✪ relations with local, regional, and national authorities.

All of these are built upon the sum of what you do and how you do it.

A company brand, like a product brand or personal brand, must deliver on its promises. It must meet a relevant need, provide relevant solutions, and remove relevant pain. It must do no harm—and try to do good—starting with real-world, rubber-meets-the-road customer relationship management ... as opposed to the check-the-boxes "corporate citizenship" measures trotted out in recent years.

Leesa Sleep (leesa.com) sells mattresses online. This start-up, founded by our friends David Wolfe and Jamie Dimondstein, has disrupted the mattress industry by removing the uncomfortable, unreliable, and very expensive in-store marketing funnel approach developed by department stores and branded mattress stores—apparently to create a quintessential smoke-and-mirrors shopping experience. Leesa Sleep has benefitted from the years of advertising by Tempurpedic and other luxury foam mattress makers, but the company doesn't do any traditional advertising itself. Instead, it offers to replace the traditional purchase experience of mattress and department stores with a 100-night guarantee. More than any ad or testimonial could do, this promises satisfaction and proclaims total confidence in product and usage experience.

That will get you to order the mattress, pain-free, smoke-free, mirror-free. The industry-disrupting purchase experience continues upon delivery. The mattress, which retails at less than half the price of a Tempurpedic, is "built to order and shipped within 3 to 5 business days." The mattress is delivered (free) in a box. The "unboxing" experience is a shared secret of Leesa Sleep's early-adopter customers. It's often shared on video in social media. Un-box the Leesa Sleep mattress, and it unfolds into a very comfortable, high-quality king mattress. Okay. So it unfolds. Actually, it does more. In unfolding, its 100% American-made molecular structure actually changes.

And if that's not enough to distinguish the brand, for every mattress sold, Leesa plants a tree. Sounds okay, but sounds even better when you realize the scope of this program. Leesa has "out-planted" the global Google tree-planting effort. For every ten mattresses sold, Leesa donates a mattress to a homeless shelter. And, at this writing, three New York City shelters are fully outfitted with donated Leesa mattresses, with many more on the way to shelters around the country and soon around the world. David Wolfe's commitment to start-up as not only "for profit," but also "for purpose," has given the brand authenticity and relevance for its young, socially and politically active customers.

The Leesa brand sells the benefits of sleep more than the benefits of mattresses. That is what the 100-night risk-free trial tells you. The brand targets young, highly connected consumers. Instead of advertising, social media broadcasts customer satisfaction—and any customer problems—far and wide and at digital speed. The result is a consistent and consistently insurgent brand narrative that aligns product, package, purchase experience, guarantee, and social agenda in ways that are all relevant to the target audience.

Alignment of all strategies and all communications is a necessary goal for coherent and compelling brand development.

Leesa's leaders have made sure you know what they do and how they do it—and then every expression of these factors in distribution, branding, packaging, logos, advertising, PR, corporate citizenship, CRM, and employee relations are lined up like the Rockettes at Christmas. Try it. It works.

Alignment adds power to the meaning of your company. This creates the power of focus and repetition, the repetition of your meaning in many channels and many different forms of expression.

In today's corporate fishbowl, what *can* be known *will* be known. Never forget this. Continuity communicates authenticity and develops credibility. Yes, people will see your philanthropic acts and may appreciate them, but today's informed audiences will be quick to wonder what might be hiding just beneath any veneer of philanthropy. We think, in fact, that stakeholder access is like peeling an onion. Some will be satisfied with the most superficial information. Others will peel and peel to get at the information they want. And making the truth hard to access or difficult to understand won't stop those willing to seek it. All it will do is piss them off—and you don't want that.

For example, as part of our work for a big packaged-goods company, we were asked to determine if the corporation's quite impressive, long-standing, and very large contributions to charitable and civic acts had any meaning for their Hard Support and Soft Support customers, some of whom were beginning to weaken in usage and loyalty. So we listed the firm's good deeds, presented the list to consumers, and received a remarkably uniform response: "That's good. They're a big, rich corporation. They *should* be doing good things."

Then they'd think for a moment and ask, "And why are they telling me this?"

Behind this question was the assumption that the communication of these high-minded civic acts was like the magician's "misdirection," the "look-over-there" stage performance tactic intended to transform an actual trick into a perceived miracle. Such is the cynicism of today's information consumers. Don't blame them. Blame marketing. For generations now, marketers have taught consumers to suspect and expect the worst.

Yes, your company should do good things in the community in line with the leaders' and employees' sense of corporate responsibility and the needs of the communities in which you work and live. Even better, encourage civic action and volunteering within the company. It's not just a good demonstration of your good intentions; it's a good way to connect your employees to the real people who are usually seen as percentage points in the market analyses.

The phrase "doing well by doing good" became popular in the 1990s and 2000s. It was something of a self-conscious admission that the norm in the corporate world was doing bad or, at least, no better than the law said you had to do. Creating products with integrity, honest customer relationships, jobs, salaries, profits, taxes, and shareholder returns does plenty of good. Those are the most important things to your customers and community, too. Philanthropy and community action are the cherry on the icing on the cake. **First, bake the cake. Do well by doing well.**

Given today's very savvy and very cynical consumers, corporate advertising can be a dicey proposition. The famous—or infamous—result of Mobil's corporate ads, vintage 1980s, was to associate Mobil with all the negativity toward "oil companies"—before they renamed themselves "energy companies"—in the dawning age of environmentalism. Basically, the ads backfired by making Mobil the tallest midget in town. Taking a shot at asking people to love you for your good heart and kind intentions is likelier to hit you in your corporate foot rather than find a viable consumer target.

Nevertheless, informing stakeholders about what you do and how you do it is good. We see such communications more often in paid media these days. Most citizens' first awareness of the Koch brothers is through political news punditry, where they are often portrayed as dark forces on the political landscape. "Who the hell *are* these people?" was the pervasive question raised by the mainstream press. (The answer seemed to be somewhere between Mr. Burns of *The Simpsons* and Darth Vader of *Star Wars*). The "We are Koch" ads are not creative or elegant, but simply let consumers know that a lot of everyday products and everyday working people are behind the Koch name.

Build your corporate brand around an honest communication of what you do and how you do it. The best corporate advertising is also built inside-out in the knowledge that actions always out-broadcast advertising.

Creating a Change Culture Inside-Out

Long before you are asked to lead a division, region, or company, you will be asked to lead a project. Yes, as project leader, you want to make sure you define the problem clearly and then solve it. You want to under-promise and over-deliver. You want to own your results. And you also want to begin a change culture within the team you lead. Why do you want this? It is the viral beginning of shaping the culture of the entire company.

Set some ground rules in advance:

1. Never accept, "We do it that way, because that's the way we've always done it."

2. Deliberately violate corporate rituals and confront the embedded fear of change that rests at the core of most corporations.

3. Change the rules. Change, in fact, is the great fear. So run right at it.

4. As a team, agree on the definition of the problem. Then develop hypotheses of solutions—no holds barred. This is not about building consensus, but creating an open development platform and challenging status quo approaches. Doing this gives everyone on the team ownership of the eventual strategic approach. "Silence means thunderous approval," is a useful warning to encourage vocal participation.

5. In developing the strategy for the project, take chances without being truly reckless. Use strategy to play more offense.

6. Help your team play by the rules of insurgents, with "do the doable" objectives that will help establish momentum. Insist on defining "move the movable" targets internally and externally for that strategy.

7. Know the "votes" you need to move in order to win.

8. Always play offense. Never play defense. Never compromise your own principles for consensus. Instead, pull your team's ideas into the process as much as possible. From that moment on, strategy becomes boss.

9. Make it *our* strategy, not your strategy. People who get things done by taking over and just seeing it through on their own are invaluable employees, but lousy leaders. Be a great employee *and* a great leader.

Participation in developing strategic and tactical plans builds a stronger team effort to make those strategies and plans work. Recognition and reward for special effort are also important. Use praise, criticism, *and* goodies to reinforce change culture. Be consistent. Reward taking the initiative, playing offense. This may mean rewarding mistakes of commission, because they are the mistakes of "going for it." A rare occasion may call for a public hanging of a team member who acts dishonestly or with complete disregard for his/her teammates. More usually, any situation requiring "correction" can be dealt with privately. Be clear in expressing the problem, and then hope it's a learning opportunity and not a pixel in a pattern of bad acting.

Always Communicate Inside-Out

Whether it's to your team or to your company, remember the importance of communicating inside-out. The rule gets violated when management is excited or scared. Often, when making an announcement of good news—a positive development in markets, a merger, or acquisition—management will rush outside for the announcement to the *Wall Street Journal*, a juicy interview on CNBC, or a press conference to analysts and shareholders. The same happens in crisis, or when negative news is being announced. Doors are closed on the executive floor. Lots of hushed talking in the halls. The employees are the last to know. Clueless employees are slower, more cynical, and have their antennas up for other opportunities. They have to use their imagination to figure out what's happening, and that always leans toward the negative.

When they (meaning all of your "friends and family": employees, alumni, suppliers, market partners, and Hard Support customers, shareholders, analysts, and influencers) feel they are on the inside of the information, they will be more likely to support it, to tune into the strategy behind it, and to help spread your key messages to other audiences.

There wasn't a hell of a lot to be proud of on either side in the government's antitrust assault on Microsoft in the 2000s. It was a political positioning action on the part of the government—and particularly the prosecutor, Joel Klein. Microsoft was the poster child (as Michael Milken and Drexel, Burnham, Lambert had been a decade before) for what the Clinton administration considered big business excesses. (BTW: Outsized contributions to The Clinton Foundation have never been considered a big business excess.)

We helped our long-time client Microsoft, though the effort was made more challenging by the attitude of then-CEO Bill Gates. He kept repeating the same mantra: "We're right. They're wrong. We'll win." The mistake Bill made was assuming the case was about justice when, in fact, it was about politics. Sure, Microsoft had the facts on their side. That made little difference in the eventual settlement with the Department of Justice. Bill's deaf ear to the political music was the downfall of Microsoft in the public eye. (As the DOJ and Securities and Exchange Commission saw it, the case was decided before it started.) Still, one battle was won in that campaign. We recommended that Microsoft adopt a program we called "friends & family," naming it after MCI's insurgent assault on AT&T. Having looked at internal research interviews, we realized that the employees of Microsoft, their suppliers, partners, large corporate customers, and other supporters were under constant personal attack for their taking Microsoft's side. Employees were confronted at neighborhood barbecues, at industry events, even on planes when their seatmates would see the Microsoft business card on their briefcase.

"How can you work with those thugs?!"

We felt we had to help furnish Microsoft with the weapons it needed to defend itself. First, this was necessary to keep up the flagging morale of the Microsoft work force. Second, their defending themselves effectively meant they would be defending Microsoft effectively.

We provided every employee and other stakeholder with basic "3x5 card" messages in support of Microsoft's positioning, as well as the facts supporting those messages. There was also a commitment to make sure the "friends & family" would get any new facts or new developments first, before the public. Microsoft's steady growth through the government's war against them is proof of the program's effect. The insiders stayed with the company. That made enough of a difference to make all the difference at the time.

One last point from politics: **Loyalty in politics is not developed by what you give, but by what you ask.** Yes, that sounds crazy. The Democrats and Republicans are forever promising their constituents this or that government giveaway. Still, the facts are the facts, and we've seen them repeated for thirty-some years of political campaigns around the world. Asking a supporter to do something for you, like asking a member of your core strategy group to contribute to developing strategy, gives him/her a piece of the project and a stake in its success or failure. Asking a supporter to do you a favor cements their loyalty. Autocrats always ask their closest allies to kill someone for them. That's the ultimate sacrifice and the Gorilla Glue of political affiliation. Weird, yes. But still true.

You may be the kind of leader who would rather take on the most difficult challenges solo. But that's robbing your team of the opportunity to prove their own worth to you and to themselves. Ask for help. Ask for contributions to the cause. Let us remind you of how we developed a definition of corporate culture with Bob Iger at Disney:

✪ "I'm a part of something great."

✪ "I can make a difference."

✪ "Somebody recognizes the difference I make."

Being a part of it is important. And having the opportunity to make a difference is the hope of every employee. As Nike says, "Just Do It." Give them a chance to make the winning contribution.

★ Step 5 ★
ANNOUNCE Your Candidacy

Develop your stump speech, define the change you represent, resolve to play offense.

We've all seen it so many times, we can instantly paint the picture in our minds. The groomed and coifed candidate at the podium, smiling, waving, pointing to somebody in the crowd he doesn't even know. Behind the podium, a rainbow coalition of smiling, cheering people, fitting exactly the campaign's target demographics. Red, white, and blue bunting all over the place, and red, white, and blue balloons soon to fall from the net above the stage. Off to one side, the candidate's spouse and their children, very presentable and very uncomfortable. The new logo and "YOUR NAME GOES HERE for President" sign are both stuck onto the podium and behind the candidate.

Here it comes. The announcement—a surprise to no one and a piece of political theater as old as the Republic.

As long as the teleprompter functions correctly, everything will go as planned.

"Today, I announce my candidacy for President of the United States!"

Cue balloons.

The political announcement has ritualistic certainty to it. In the business world, however, it's a lot less certain and far from ritualistic. These days, in fact, it's pretty much up for grabs.

A. "I've put in my time. I've been a senior vice president for six years, for Chrissake!"

B. "Dave promised me I'd be the next CEO."

C. "I've been working on the key board members for the past two years. I'm a shoo-in."

D. "I'm the one who can continue Dave's strategies and vision for the company."

E. "It's *my* turn."

Or maybe—F: "None of the above."

So-called orderly succession is a thing of the past in the corporate world—and, you know what, from now on probably in the political world, too. Going forward, we expect that virtually every succession is going to be disorderly and disruptive.

Why do we say this?

Just take a look at our presidential political campaigns. Either you disrupt your leadership status quo, or a competitor will do it for you. When they do, it will hardly matter to you, because by then you'll be so far out into the icy Atlantic that the first lifeboats will have already departed. Boards of directors are beginning to understand this simple reality. So every transition is up in the air.

As we say, "The molecules are in motion." And that means change—with a capital "C" that rhymes with "T" and that stands for … Tums Extra Strength. This is causing the Mother of All Heartburn for boards of directors everywhere. Today, even the most successful CEOs don't leave a "cruise control" strategy behind—the metaphorical folded note of the past that had but a single sentence: "Just don't change a thing."

It just doesn't work anymore.

The next CEO of your company, like the next president of the United States, must represent change and create change—or, when running for re-election, will represent "unfinished change." This is because we live in a change environment with disruptive forces affecting every market, every sector, every community, and every country. The pervasive, all-consuming information environment is the engine of this change environment, and if you don't credibly change with it, you will be incredibly changed by it.

This is not just the situation for companies already in crisis. Even to keep a successful organization on its successful tack will take change to avoid pop-up obstacles and exploit pop-up opportunities alike. That's why government is both inept and corrupt. It was designed by the Founders with the very best of intentions, by which they meant constant change, what Jefferson outspokenly hoped would be a continuing American Revolution. But from the first set of governing incumbents forward for 240 years, those in place didn't want to leave, and so they tried to establish a system immune to change. *Change or be changed? No to both, young fella!*

So at least we already know what your leadership campaign theme will be: change. That's what it *has* to be. But what if *your* company is not interested in changing with changing times? Start looking to lead *another* company.

In this, the Age of Disorderly Succession, you cannot wait your turn. Expect the inevitable to happen and it will not happen, inevitably. You have to go for it, even if you have to leave for it.

What does *that* "announcement event" look like?

It *looks* like your whole career, at least from the moment you begin to exhibit leadership qualities or characteristics and, more specifically, when your performance begins to demonstrate that you know how to lead people and how to accomplish goals. So the "event" is really a process. In business, you have thrown your hat in the ring when you either decide to start that process or when you decide to make the most of it.

As we've said before, not everybody wants to be a leader. That's fine. Really, it is. There are many rewarding, creative, and remunerative roles in business and, for that matter, in government, that do not call for candidacy. But if you want to be a leader, you cannot wait to be discovered, like Lana Turner, by sitting on a stool in Schwab's Drugstore. Leadership will not be handed to you. Some leaders—especially political leaders—relish the fiction that greatness was thrust upon them, that they had no choice but to lead, that it's what The People demanded .... But this *is* a fiction, the very same fiction a good car salesman creates to persuade you that the car *she* is selling you is the car *you* wanted all along. No, leadership is not given. It is earned and, ultimately, taken. If you want to lead, start leading right away.

Every Company Needs All the Leaders It Can Find

We don't know your company. But we do know it needs leadership. Our experience tells us that only about 5% of all companies of all sizes and shapes have strong, visionary leaders. If you read the news, you can't help but conclude that there's a global leadership shortage. It's critical and it's at every level of corporations and governments alike, not just at the tippity-top. But, at the same time, there are some very good ones:

✪ Tim Cook had to be ready for leadership when Steven Jobs became too ill to continue as CEO. He couldn't just continue every one of Jobs's strategies, however. Things in tech have been changing too fast.

✪ William Clay Ford knew enough to know he needed an outsider to save his family's namesake company from the financial calamities of 2008. That was Boeing's former CEO, Alan Mulally.

✪ Satya Nadella has brought the product-focused leadership that Microsoft had lacked under Steve Ballmer. It was necessary change, maybe just in time.

✪ A terrific leader at eBay, Meg Whitman doesn't seem to have been the outsider needed to save Hewlett-Packard. But, then, the HP board of directors seems to be a leadership-free zone.

Your company needs leadership. Your community needs leadership. Our country, like every other country on earth, needs people who run toward trouble, not away from it. We need people with the ability to rally others to a great cause. We need people with a vision of a better future. Unfortunately, the great majority of companies and communities and countries don't get the leadership they need. That's what makes true leaders sing out so clearly from the background noise of mediocrity.

And, sure, it's great to be tall, or have a commanding voice, or be super intelligent and quick-witted. DNA helps, but the fact is that there are very few born leaders. The rest of us learn it. (We think that's why you're reading this book.) In our experience, the great ones who learn leadership never stop learning it, even when they are teaching it to others. The United States military, the finest in the history of the world, continually creates proof that leadership can be taught—and taught with reliable, often spectacular, results.

Hey, Your Hat's in the Ring!

The instant you decide to pursue leadership, even with the first project you are assigned to lead, *you* have thrown your hat in the ring for CEO at some point in the future. You may or may not realize this, but your friends, mentors, and enemies are keenly aware of it. *They* have their eye on the ring. *They* see your hat in it. So, now what?

For years we have heard company managers, motivational speakers, and coaches exhort people to "Act like a leader!"

If you want to be like a leader, act like one. Sounds like good common sense. Albert Einstein, who led physics into the future that is today, once quipped, "Common sense is the collection of prejudices acquired by age eighteen." The problem with the injunction to "act like a leader" is that it is finally advice to act like the people acting like leaders act.

Here's an important point: Leaders don't act.

We once addressed an entire coliseum-full of McDonald's owner/operators. "All your business life, you've been told to act like a leader," we began.

McDonald's is a leader, after all. You've got a heritage of terrific leaders going back to your founder, Ray Kroc. But, please, for the sake of your customers, your employees, and your company, DO *NOT* ACT LIKE A LEADER!

Leaders act like they are hard of hearing good advice. Leaders act like they have been anointed number one for life. Leaders think they have to dress like, talk like, walk like, and quack like all the leaders who came before them in the company and in the industry.

Please don't do that. That's not how Ray Kroc got to be a leader.

Act the way Ray Kroc did *on the way to* leadership. Act like you need *every* customer's business *every* time they begin to feel the first slight pangs of hunger. Act like you want to deserve their business in a marketplace filled with lots and lots of alternative options. Act like you need the very best employees and you need the very best from every employee. Act like you think you have to work harder than anybody else in the company. And act like you've got the most exciting and interesting job on the planet.

Then people will want to follow you. And then you won't have to act like a leader. You will *be* one … just like Ray Kroc.

To put this another way, **act like the leader you are *going* to be**. This is the best advice we can give anyone *on the way* to leadership. And by "act," we mean *act* as in "*act*ion." Do it:

- ✪ Act like someone customers can trust.
- ✪ Act like someone employees and shareholders can trust.
- ✪ Act like someone who can be trusted to lead people forward against all odds and take on the criticism and not just the accolades.

If you can act like this, it won't be acting.

Asking for It

To repeat: The world needs leaders. If this seems obvious—too obvious to say and certainly too obvious to repeat—that's because most of the world is already acutely aware of the need. The good news in this is that most of the people who *should* get the chance to lead *do* get the chance. The bad news is that a lot of people who *should not* under any circumstances get the chance also get the chance. In the end—we repeat—only about 5% of companies actually get great change leader visionary CEOs. The others? They get by. Or not. Far too many get a lot less leader than they need.

While we're repeating ourselves on the subject of leadership, let's say it again. Do you want to be a leader? Well, *go for it!*

Swell! How?

The fact that very few people get the chance to ask for the top job doesn't stop plenty of them from asking for it again and again and again. Occasionally, an executive recruiter may call you to ask if you'd be interested in a leadership job at another company. At the least flattered and at the most visibly salivating, you embark on a series of interviews the recruiter has arranged. Somewhere in this series, you may feel moved to indicate that you want the job. So, ask already.

Just understand that it's far better if *they* ask you—although this does not mean they hand you the reins of leadership. As we've said, this doesn't happen.

You *will* be asked, however, if your hat is already in the ring, if you have already announced your candidacy—announced it with the very first project *you* run or the first team *you* lead. Spend your career leading—not aspiring to leadership—and demonstrating your success in the process, and then you will not have to ask for it.

Leadership? Ask for the project, ask for the team, ask for the challenge, and then keep asking for bigger challenges. That's how you ask for the biggest leadership job. That's how you ask to be CEO—not with a phrase or a sentence or an interview, but with everything you do. And it will take years.

Insurgent Leadership: The Missing Manual

In Step 4 we talked about leading inside-out, about shaping an insurgent culture as you lead people in particular projects or groups. Each time you lead a team toward insurgency, you prepare for the ultimate leadership job you will have.

As we said in Step 3, revolutions don't come with user's manuals, yet we have found, over and over again, that the leaders of successful revolutions build on the same basic principles as they make their way to their win. And the next best thing to an insurgent manual is our list of insurgent principles—because when it comes to building a foundation for success in a change environment, you cannot go wrong if you use them.

1. Structure every project and every challenge as a political campaign

We talk about this throughout this book, but the overriding principle is the core characteristic of a political campaign:

- Formulate a campaign strategy to win by a certain date.
- Drive the campaign with an urgency to get the 50.1% you need to win.

These are powerful insurgent principles. They are necessary to creating a successful campaign strategy, but not alone sufficient to doing so. Your campaign strategy must be shaped by the unique form of the particular challenge at hand:

- Develop this strategy with your team.
- Start by clearly defining the destination of your project and the terms of the success you will achieve in getting there. Again, we call this *defining the win*.

- Create your definition with the purpose of marshaling your resources carefully. As described, we call this *doing the doable*.

- To do the doable, you will first need to identify the targets—and only these targets—you need to win over in order to succeed. We call this again *moving the movable*.

- Now, develop compelling logic and magnetic messaging that allows more and more people to adopt your strategy and make it their strategy. This is what we mean by *building your campaign inside-out*.

- Relentlessly and continuously fight for control of the dialogue. This is *playing offense, never playing defense*.

2. Define the change you will bring

Today, leading is communicating. Each project you lead and every challenge you take on defines your leadership style and character. You must, therefore, become adept at developing compelling messaging to go along with your compelling campaign strategy.

We assume you agree that your leadership will stand for change. Every project you lead is a part of your leadership campaign in the same way that every debate and every straw poll and every primary is part of a candidate's long, long presidential campaign. The most important thing you will communicate in every project is the *kind* of change you represent.

About your *personal brand* we said, the *but* and the *and* often introduce the most important attributes: "She is a dynamic leader"—

"*but* there are interpersonal issues she has to overcome."

or

"*and* she is a hell of a team builder."

About *change* as it relates to your leadership brand, the key words are not *but* and *and*, but *from* and *to*. *From* is all about the problems that exist with the status quo, whether it is a hidebound bureaucracy or a failure to address a changing marketplace. *To* is where you are going, the kind of company you are going to be.

Go to your journal and write a list of *from/to* statements about the project you are working on. For instance:

"*from* reactive to consumer complaints about X"

"*to* a proactive and interactive CRM strategy."

You get it. It's the whole point of change. Change should be to a *better* state. Here's where we are, and there's where we're going.

From/to is a good way to state the objectives of your leadership campaign, and, along with the problem/solution model, it is a good way to state the objectives of any project. You remind your communications targets of the problems of the status quo (*from*) and the promise of your active change campaign (*to*)—what *your* strategies will achieve.

3. Develop 3x5 card discipline

From/to is an ideal structure for your essential leadership communications. The paradigm will also help you master the 3x5 card messaging principle and help you develop your basic stump speech. Both are foundational communications elements of any campaign and for any leader.

You've seen it so often that you probably barely notice it any longer. As the president walks to the podium, he/she pulls an index card or two from his/her coat pocket. These days, it's the same in almost every country and at almost every podium. The 3x5 card is the essential element of a successful campaign, because it states the campaign's strategy in a framework that can be easily communicated by any number of people within and in support of the administration. It is specific, and yet it is easily adopted to the personal communications style of everyone in the campaign.

The 3x5 card consists of:

- ✪ A headline, which states the principal objective of the campaign strategy.

- ✪ Four or five bullet points, which define the support for that strategic objective: how we'll attain our objective.

- ✪ The bulleted *support points* that define for all stakeholders the relevant benefits in the campaign.

- ✪ The bulleted *support points* that define how you will differentiate the strategy in your marketplace.

- ✪ The bulleted *support points* that define the better future that will result from the campaign's success.

The rules of 3x5 card messaging are simple:

- ✪ The 3x5 card is the basic campaign communications framework.

- ✪ It reflects the core strategy and, to be effective, it must be consistently communicated by everyone involved with the campaign.

- ✪ All the points of the 3x5 card will be communicated to everyone.

- ✪ For use by any particular group in any particular situation, a team member may drill down on one or more of the points in greater depth; however, each team member will always communicate all the points on the 3x5 card in every situation.

If the campaign idea expressed in 3x5 card discipline is compelling—if its *from/to* describes a shining city on the hill—it will spread like Bird Flu. It will spread from your team to others in the organization, and to suppliers and partners and your loyal customers and all others who will be affected by the campaign.

But make sure the primary focus is on those who will have the biggest impact on the campaign's success. It is repetition of basic themes and messages that charges them with the power of conviction. So run the wheels off your basic 3x5 card messaging before even thinking of altering it.

4. Develop a stump speech

Like all communications from and about the campaign, the stump speech is developed from the 3x5 card framework. As we recounted in showing you Bob Iger's 3x5 card and stump speech from 2005, it should be above all else simple, direct, and clear. If you add clever touches, terrific, but never at the expense of simplicity, directness, and clarity.

"What's a good joke I can start with?" you ask. (No, you don't, do you?) To us, a good joke is starting yet another speech with a joke-book joke. It's like saying, "Good morning!" and cupping your hand to your ear for the response from an audience that is wincing in embarrassment.

No one in history, ancient or modern, has improved on Aristotle's three-part advice concerning composition, which boils down to—

A. Tell them what you are going to tell them.

B. Tell them.

C. Tell them what you told them.

The people you want to reach and to move with your stump speech don't need to be entertained. This is serious stuff to them. Put the joke book back on the toilet tank where you took it from and stick to Aristotle.

  ✪ Deliver the 3x5 card messages.

  ✪ Add detail, relevant examples, interesting facts, and even a dash of wit and charm.

  ✪ Just keep it simple and keep it on plan.

The stump speech is venue-agnostic. It can be a graduation speech, a shareholders' speech, a retirement party toast, a pep talk, a eulogy, a convocation address. Whatever. By all means, adapt the speech to the situation and the audience, but never, ever, change the strategy in a misguided attempt to suit a particular venue.

The stump speech strategy is set in stone until you and your team decide it must be changed. Long after you are sick of giving the same stump speech, it will just be starting to touch your key targets.

Our political candidate clients often snap at us, "People are sick of hearing that same old thing." What they forget is that the movable targets you need to motivate will never get sick of hearing messages that are relevant to their needs and wants. I mean, do you ever get sick of hearing the hiss of the foamer when you're getting that first morning cup of coffee at Starbucks?

- ✪ Repetition is consistency.
- ✪ Consistency is conviction.
- ✪ Conviction is authenticity.
- ✪ Authenticity is imperative.

"I don't really need a speech coach, do I?" you ask. And that one is a very good question, especially since it has an absolute answer: Yes, you do.

You need the best speech coach you can afford. The *best* will not be giving you a bunch of tips and tricks on how to sound like the latest TED Talk. The *best* will teach you how to be the *best you* in front of an audience. Look, leadership takes learning. Leaders take coaching well. So get the best coaches to help you be the best leader you can be. This advice extends to mentors, the cast of your Kitchen Cabinet, and your company's current leadership.

5. Insurgent leaders are fit to lead

They say you can't judge a book by its cover. So why do books have covers? Well, we *all* judge books by their covers. Their function is to guide our judgment of the book.

In defining your personal brand, you want the imagery of a member of Airborne Ranger Special Forces: ready to jump into any kind of trouble anytime, anywhere. Our friend Captain Stu Gallagher has his unit's motto inscribed everywhere: "*Si vis pacem, para bellum.*" "If you want peace, prepare for war."

The way you take on challenges great and small ultimately defines for others the kind of leader you will be. Guide that definition with personal imagery that broadcasts physical fitness—with emphasis on *fitness*, the capacity and suitability to lead.

It's not just about the imagery of a rough and ready leader. Leadership today is often described as a marathon, not a sprint. Actually, it's more like a triathlon or a decathlon, calling for multiple skills, all of which require strength, stamina, and determination. Get fit to lead.

Even the Green Berets we know don't go to the extremes of fitness Johnson & Johnson CEO Alex Gorsky embraces. At fifty-four, he's in the gym with his wife, Pat, by 5:30 every morning that he's home, kicking off a ninety-minute workout that would challenge any pro athlete. He keeps up the same pace on the road. J&J's Human Performance Institute has developed an Executive Athlete program based on the principle that managing energy is more important than managing time for today's executive leaders. Alex leads by example at J&J and has defined wellness and prevention as the next and most important frontier in healthcare. After all, the best medicine is avoiding disease and injury in the first place.

Energy affects attitude and aptitude—as you go through your day and through your career. Keeping fit physically keeps you sharp mentally and emotionally. The discipline of personal fitness is one of many that you'll need to master in the leadership campaign. Consider it the foundation of those other disciplines, and you'll be a better leader in them all.

Campaigning is strenuous. You need all of your strength to start and to sustain the effort. Equally important, nothing announces the strength and discipline befitting a leader more clearly and eloquently than a flesh-and-blood image of strength and discipline conveyed live and in person.

✪ Step 6 ✪
DEFINE Everything

Define yourself, your target constituencies, the stakes,
the enemy, the win, the future.

The sound is something like a hand lawn-mower: "chicka-chicka-chicka-chicka." Only this is a hundred of them going all at the same time over the same lawn. It's almost deafening. And the lights trained right into your eyeballs are totally blinding. And if you hadn't heard it before and been blinded by it in dozens of other press conferences, the whole thing would rattle the brains out of you. Camera shutters clicking, TV lights glaring.

Who's out there?

You know very well.

You can't see beyond the lights, and you can't hear above the snapping shutters, but you know the room is full. And you know very well what it's full of ....

The reporters are elbowing for position so their camera crews can shoot you, then cut to the reporter asking a gotcha question, and then move on to broadcast set up with the reporter on camera and the press conference in the background: "In ... Davenport, Iowa, ... this is ... Chuck Todd ... NBC ... News."

The reporters jostle to get their questions answered. Each has a list of twenty—times the eighty to a hundred reporters ... so let's say sixteen hundred questions are attached to the forest of raised hands waving in the pools of light.

Sixteen hundred questions!

But if you know politics, you know there are really only two questions that demand answering today.

Number one is *Who the hell are you?*

Number two is *Why the hell are you running for president?*

In any case, you're not here for questions. You're here to give the answers you want to give.

Full disclosure: There are more than two questions that demand immediate answers. There are seven—and you better prepare answers to all of them, answers good enough to last out your entire campaign for president of the United States— or president of [*fill in your country*] or CEO of [*fill in your company*].

Seven Definitions

Seven answers is all you need—assuming, of course, there was no dalliance with an intern and your briefcase isn't stuffed with large-denomination, unmarked bills. We call these seven answers the "Seven Definitions." They are:

1. This is who I am.

2. These are my target voters (those I absolutely have to move, and those who are movable).

3. This is the win (and how these target voters will feel, think, and behave differently as a result of the win).

4. These are the stakes in this election (in other words, why your targets should give a shit about your candidacy).

5. Why you should give me money or tie your future success to me.

6. This is the enemy of our mutual win.

7. This is the future I want to lead us to.

Remember, these are not seven *potential* questions. **They are the seven you-bet-your-ass-and-career definitions you must control and communicate if you are going to have a shot at a successful campaign.**

You can answer questions about exchange rates or the supply chain or commodity prices if you really want to. Those answers may earn you an A on a term paper, but they won't get you into the top office. It's all about the seven.

One: This Is Who I Am

We'll tell you what we always tell candidates: **You must clearly and compellingly define yourself, or others will be happy to do the job for you.**

We talked about this in the "The Brand of You" section back in Step 1. The point is it's vital that you take control of defining who you are. And, remember, this is not an online dating site. What will actually count most is the authenticity of you.

Another thing we say over and over: What *can* be known *will* be known. That's the absolute rule of the Google age. You may think you have one little secret that nobody knows and nobody can *possibly* know. But *somebody*, somewhere, somehow knows it, or *can* know it with enough digital digging. (And since it's *digital* digging, anybody can do it.)

The attraction of the "outsider," non-political political candidates for 2016 is the popular assumption of authenticity. Voters are willing to cut outsiders a break by assuming the authenticity they present really is authentic. It is not an assumption they make in the case of professional politicians. Quite the contrary. If you've been a lifelong politician, you got some 'splainin' to do. In the French legal system, you are presumed guilty until you prove your innocence. In the American political system, you—as a professional politician—are assumed inauthentic until you prove your authenticity. The same holds true if you are a candidate for corporate leadership who's come up through the ranks in your company. Today, people don't trust big institutions and the insiders who run them.

In 2015, we became involved, along with Patrick Caddell and Bob Perkins, in what we call "We Need Smith" (http://weneed-smith.com/), a movement to support new leaders and new ideas from outside the broken Washington system. Much of our work in this movement consisted of research that revealed the genuinely historic levels of frustration, anger, and alienation among all voters. We are all aware that young urban African Americans are afraid of the police, angry at them, and frustrated by the lack of change in the situation. That's how 85%-plus of *all* Americans feel about our government in Washington.

And they don't feel any warmer of belly when it comes to corporate leadership.

In fact, when you present yourself as candidate for CEO, you are going to face a six-foot-high wall of cynicism with broken glass embedded in the top. **So here comes our next political lesson: The most powerful form of propaganda in the solar system is the truth.** There is a reason H. K. McCann, founder of the iconic McCann-Erickson ad agency, defined good advertising as "Truth well told." Tell the truth. Tell it well. But tell the truth. It's not only the moral high ground and the right thing to do. It will also save you a lot of time and a lot of heartburn.

Telling the truth and telling it well means finding a way to flush *corporatespeak* from your vocabulary. For instance—

"Our associates" is corporatespeak for "the people who work here."

"However" is really "but."

"Core competency" should be "what we do better than anybody."

"Buy-in" is simply "agreement."

"Empower" should be "expect" or "demand" or "require."

"Move the needle" should be "improve" or "succeed" or "win."

"Lots of moving parts" should be "I will deliver it by the end of the day."

"Make hay" should be "Just do it."

"Scalable" really means "capable of growth and therefore worth doing"—this takes more words, but at least everyone understands them and can't evade their meaning.

"Best practice" really means "what everybody else does"—so is that really what you want to do, you plagiarizing drone, you?

"Think outside the box" is really "innovate."

"Ducks in a row" is actually "Make a frickin' plan, why don't you?"

"Ecosystem" is industry or marketplace or whatever context you really need to invoke in order to make yourself understood instead of ignored by people who correctly shut their eyes, ears, hearts, and minds at the first whiff of horse pucky.

"Leverage" can usually be replaced by "manage."

"Vertical" means "area of expertise." (Unless you are referring to the opposite of *horizontal.*)

"Full service" is a meaningless substitute for specifying what you and your firm actually do.

"Drill down" suggests agony, whereas "study" implies enlightenment.

"It is what it is" is stupid. Instead, specify the facts of the matter at hand and what you're going to do about them.

"Robust" seems like a euphemism for "morbidly obese."

"Take offline" means "postpone" or, worse, "put off."

"Synergize" is "cooperate" or "collaborate," much as "expectorate" is "spit" and "micturate" is "urinate."

"Learnings" are "lessons."

"Reach out" is "contact."

"Punt" is really "give up."

"Impact," as a verb, stinks. Say "affect."

"Give 110%" means nothing to people in business who actually measure cost and benefit.

"Price point" is "price."

"Take it to the next level" should be "improve it."

"Cut and dry" should be "settled" or "easy" or "simple" or "boring" or whatever else your lazy ass means.

"Out of pocket" should be "I won't be here" or "I'm traveling then" or "I'll be washing my hair" or whatever reason you need to give for being unavailable.

"Window of opportunity" is better handled with "our only chance," "deadline," or "urgent."

"Low-hanging fruit" is an "easy win."

"Peel the onion" is "understand the complexity."

"Corporate values" must never be confused with "core values."

When you are defining who you are, don't spout a list of accomplishments. You are a leader, not a CV. Some people like history, but few are compelled by it. They will be interested in what *you have done*, but only *after* they know *who you are*.

Think about it. You're at a cocktail party. You meet some stranger. He starts talking about all the things he's done, places he's been, people he's met. And all the time you're wondering: "Who the hell is this person?"

People want to know *how* you decide things more than what you *have* decided or say that you *will* decide. They want to know the character and the values that shape your decisions. If they feel confident about these, they won't worry about what you will decide. Candidates can get away with changing positions—*provided* they are honest about the reasons why. And, by the way, better add "'My position' on 'that issue has evolved'" to the list of corporatespeak because, whatever it is, it is not honest.

If you actually are a candidate reading this, you are probably thinking, "Come on, guys. I can't tell them I changed my vote on that bill because the IBEW said they'd give me $500K and an endorsement if I did. This honesty stuff only goes so far." Well, the thing is, as we've already pointed out: "What *can* be known *will* be known." And if you need another reason for telling the truth, here's what we advise candidates: "You're going to tell the truth *eventually*. The only question is, do you do it on your terms, or not?"

As the saying goes, "Tell the truth, tell it all, tell it fast." At least when you tell it on your terms and early in the relevant events, you can tell it well. The alternative, which is telling it later, with your long-suffering, but "still-supportive" spouse by your side in a tearful press conference is far from the ideal way to tell it well.

In business today, "No comment," or, even worse, just not commenting, is precisely the same as shouting "You got me! I'm guilty!" Silence is admission. Loud silence says, "Let your imagination fill in the blanks."

- ✪ Tell them who you are and what you believe.
- ✪ Tell them how you developed the value system that guides you.
- ✪ Tell them your fears, your angers, and your hopes. They want to hear it. They want to know you. So don't make them work at it.

The most effective leaders take on a simple brand positioning:

- ✪ Bob Iger at The Walt Disney Company: The Anti-Eisner
- ✪ Sergio Zyman at The Coca-Cola Company: Make shit happen
- ✪ Alex Gorsky at Johnson & Johnson: The Credo
- ✪ Steven Jobs at Apple Computer: "I am Apple" (The template statement for most founder-owners.)
- ✪ Jim Koch at Samuel Adams: The Ultimate Beer Nerd

Two: These Are My Target Voters

You're right if you think it's not always a great idea to list your "target voters." It seems a little obvious and maybe a little conniving. But if your target voters have to guess that you're talking to them, trying to reach them, and addressing their concerns, then you might as well just list them—because you must know precisely the votes you need to win.

Again, in 2005, after Michael Eisner named him the new CEO of The Walt Disney Company, Bob Iger listened to us when we said, "You've been selected. But you must be elected. All those people who felt you were foisted on them must feel like you were their idea."

It was easy for Bob to identify his "target voters." They were Walt's nephew Roy Disney and Stanley Gold, dissidents on the Disney BOD; Steven Jobs, who was also a disaffected major Disney shareholder; and all the heads of the Disney divisions, from parks to retail to movies to TV (ABC and ESPN). He worked on them, and, within six months, he really *was* their idea. And every year of Disney's remarkable success over the past decade, they are more and more convinced of how strongly they wanted Bob to be CEO all along.

Use the segmentation we described in Step 3. Again, it looks like this—on a spreadsheet, a white board, or a cocktail napkin:

HO SO UNDECIDED SS HS

HO = Hard Opposition. They hate your ass. They may be loyalists of another candidate or company, but you will also find them in your own company. A few years ago, we were working for Hewlett-Packard after they had acquired Electronic Data Systems (EDS). (HP acquired multibillion-dollar turkey tech companies the way Imelda Marcos acquired gaudy shoes.) The EDS workers in France were pissed. They kidnapped the managers. Now *that's* what we call Hard Opposition. Wherever they are, they will actively work against your interests.

So what's the good news? HO represents a very small segment of any group or any market, maybe 5–8%.

SO = Soft Opposition. They may not like you, or they may prefer another candidate/brand, but they're not really strongly committed against you. In political terms, a steady drizzle will keep them away from the polls. Still, they represent about 15–20% of the total. Just make sure the arguments of the HO don't prove motivating to these people. If HO and SO band together, you have an almost insurmountable obstacle to success.

Undecided. In mass marketing, many trillions and googles of money have been wasted on trying to win the loyalty of undecided consumers. Mass marketers love them because there are *so many* of them. We have found that in consumer markets, the undecided are undecided by character (they refuse to affiliate with one brand) or circumstances (they have to buy on price or geographical convenience). It's very hard to hold their business profitably. They are attracted to shiny objects, such as expensive new product launches. And they are irresistibly attracted to price promotion. Give them both at once, and they are in heaven. An expensive new product launch that is practically giving the product away? Well, actually, who *could* resist?

It's true that almost any brand has to count on buying its first few sales through development and manufacturing costs, distribution and marketing costs, and so on. The idea, however, is to begin to recover those losses as soon as you develop a base of loyal users, who don't demand constant novelty or the stimulation of deep discounts.

It seems that the undecided are what the lemmings have been chasing all these years. The late, great *Washington Post* political columnist Art Buchwald used to make a lot of money by speaking at corporate events. He told a story about being cornered at a cocktail hour by a young marketing executive from Procter & Gamble. The youngster was excited to tell Buchwald about a cool new product launch he was managing. "Of course," he explained, "it has been very expensive to develop. We actually lose money on every sale. But we plan to make it up on volume."

Take a look at the fast-food business. How many artery-arresting toppings of poultry, pork, cheese, chili con carne, and beef can you pile on that new burger to attract the elusive "Millennial" male? Your competitor will pile on one more layer next week, and then separate the layers with waffles injected with (ersatz) maple syrup. And *you* only have a year or two of their lives to reach them before coronary thrombosis takes them.

As a candidate for higher corporate office, you can't afford to waste your time trying to win the support of the undecided in your company. That's not to say you don't need their support. Eventually, you do. But we will soon explain the best way to move them, by and by. In the meantime, as they say in Brooklyn: fuggedaboutit!

SS = Soft Support. These are the people who like you, your candidate or brand, but just not quite *enough* to make a lasting commitment of active, vocal support. Still, you do want and need their support. First of all, like the SO, they represent about 15–20% of the available "votes." Best of all, they *want* to like you. They just need more reasons or different reasons than they've heard so far. Laser in on these people. They will make you the winner if you do. We'll tell you how that works in a minute.

HS = Hard Support. These are your invaluable loyalists. They love and support you, and they will actively and vocally try to help you/your candidate/brand win. Never, ever take the HS for granted. The same is true for your strongest fans within your company. Lavish attention on them.

In commercial markets we try to find out exactly what it is that excites the HS. What we've found in market after market is that they not only know their favorite brand better than others, but, precisely because of their familiarity with it, they also know it *differently.* They have a unique appreciation for the brand's special—or hidden—qualities. It is often the case that when others—most import, the Soft Support, who already *want* to like the brand—learn about these qualities, they see the brand in a different and better light. So this is the way that you laser in on the Soft Support. We call it "Brand Positioning According to the Hard Support." It works. In mass markets, the effect of gaining more usage and more viral testimony from the Soft Support creates the most powerful form of advertising on earth. It creates momentum in politics and business alike. There is magic in momentum, a force that will actually and eventually move some of the Undecided your way. Like the butterfly flutters that end up creating a hurricane on the other side of the earth, it all starts with the small group of your loyalists.

Though they are a small group (about 5–8%, like their opposite segment, the Hard Opposition), the HS imparts inordinate power to your brand. As we've said before, we accept the Pareto Curve as a concept, but challenge the numbers, the 20/80 Pareto number that says 20% of any marketplace will account for 80% of the volume. We find it's more like that 8% to maybe 10% (of the HS) doing that 80% of the volume. The outsized importance of the HS cannot be overstated, not by Pareto and not by us. They are gold, silver, and platinum in one beauteous brick.

And, as they say on those direct-response TV commercials for magical flat garden hoses or miraculous power screwdrivers, "But wait! There's more!" Your loyalists also enthusiastically endorse you and spread your key messages. Make sure you understand what it is they really like about you. Lean on your friends and mentors to help you attain a 360-degree understanding of your brand. Then make sure your HS can spread the 3x5 card message that is so important to your win.

Three: This Is the Win, This Is Success

Although you always want to define the election in terms of relevant benefits to the consumer/voter/employee, the people who work with you and for you must understand exactly what the win—success—will be.

In politics, nothing is easier. The win is 50.1%. It's the Oval Office. Most of the people who work for a president's election will never actually set foot there, but they know very well what it means. It's the seat of power and the culmination of all that you stand for. And winning that seat of power demands taking control of all seven definitions on the list.

In business, the win may open the door to the Corner Office, but it is far less clear to others what *your* winning the Corner Office will mean for *them*. Further complicating the vision of success is the fact that all the way down the long and winding road to the Corner Office, there will be both victories and losses in a variety of projects and challenges. These will define the leader you will be and the leadership change you represent.

For each project—for each meeting, even—define the win clearly.

- ✪ What are we trying to achieve?
- ✪ What are the metrics of success?
- ✪ What's the number we're trying to reach, and by when?
- ✪ How will stakeholders of this project or challenge feel, think, and behave differently as a result of your success?

The stakes in the election, project, or challenge will always be defined in the terms of the target voters or target consumers, but the win you are trying to achieve must be crystal clear to the people working with you to get that win. You will use the HO SO Undecided SS HS segmentation to shape the definition of the win:

- ✪ Nailing down the Hard Support loyalists
- ✪ Getting the HS to deliver your 3x5 card messages effectively
- ✪ Getting greater usage, engagement, and loyalty from the Soft Support
- ✪ Using both HS and SS to help pull some of the Undecided to your cause

Four: These Are the Stakes in This Election

"The stakes"—what are they?

- ✪ "The stakes" are the essence of why people should support you or your brand.
- ✪ They are the "Hope and Change" that won for Barack Obama in 2008 and 2012.
- ✪ They are the "It's the Economy, Stupid!" discipline that elected Bill Clinton in 1992.
- ✪ They are the "Can you say that you are better off than you were four years ago?" that put Ronald Reagan in the White House in 1980.

Lay out the stakes in the simplest terms possible. Even more important, express them in terms intensely and urgently meaningful to the "voters." Make the stakes relevant for them above all, because they absolutely, positively will *not* vote for you simply to advance you and your career.

The question in the mind and heart of every stakeholder is *What's in it for me?* Today's employees and consumers have lots and lots of choices in markets and plenty of them among potential corporate leaders—including completely ignoring current management or insisting on bringing in an outsider. (These days, stakeholders of every stripe just *love* outsiders.) What they insist on is a win-win. A win for you has to mean a win for them, and they want to know what *they* get as a result of *your* win.

Now, really, how hard is *that*? All you have to do is find out what your constituents really, really want and figure out how you are going to deliver it to them.

- ✪ "We want change and we want to have hope again."
- ✪ "It's all about getting the economy moving again."
- ✪ "I definitely don't feel like we're doing as well as we were four years ago."

Not hard at all!

Which is why we never cease to be gobsmacked and flabbergasted at how many corporate or political leadership candidates list their qualifications for leadership rather than the win-win stakes in their election. They tell you what they *have done*, not what they *will do*—for *you*.

Don't be that way. How do you get your constituents to vote for you? Just give them a reason to vote for you.

Our friend Jack MacDonough, former CEO of Miller Brewing, was hired away from Anheuser-Busch, where he had pulled off one of the most significant win-wins in the history of big-brewery beer business. He returned long-neck bottles to American beer drinkers. Today, they are the norm, but, at the time, beer drinkers were offered cans and squat little bottles. Both of these stacked more easily in distributors' warehouses. The long necks were easier for beer drinkers, but a trifle inconvenient for the distributors to handle. To Jack, it was an imbalanced equation, which he balanced by giving Joe Sixpack a win-win. *That* is what gets you elected. (And the CEO job at Miller came with a rare perk, coveted membership on the board of directors of the Green Bay Packers—for Jack, a decidedly double win!)

The stakes in the election must always be defined in a substance and context that belong to the voter, consumer, or employee. It's *their* election, not *yours*. So you have to think from their point of view first, second, and always.

Five: Why Should I Give You Money or Tie My Future Success to You?

You might find it helpful to think of the fifth point as a subpoint of the fourth because you must give your strongest supporters more than the reasons to support you defined as "The Stakes in This Election." You must also give them *additional reasons*.

Just who needs these additional reasons?

In a political election, they are your major donors, the people who provide the money you need to mount and run a winning campaign. In a campaign for corporate leadership, they are the people above and below you who will identify with you and your leadership to shape, transform, and improve the future of the company.

The primary reason to support you is that you are going to win. You persuade these supporters that you will win big by winning smaller battles on the way to the big war. When a presidential candidate is looking for a handout from a whale—a big donor—the number-one appeal is, "I am going to win, and here's why ..."

Political donors may have venal reasons for supporting a winner: "We're going to get that lower corporate tax rate!" Same goes for corporate supporters: "I'll end up with a promotion to executive VP for Supply Chain!" They may have a more noble and altruistic reason: "This is the change *we* need!" That's a reason that applies to any leadership campaign, political or corporate.

It is never a mistake to appeal to the nobility rather than the venality. The emotional effect is huge. It may, however, be a big mistake to appeal to the venality rather than the nobility. In the case of running for public political office or leadership in a public company, the mistake may even lead to a perp walk.

Six: This Is the Enemy of Our Mutual Win

What stands between you + your team and victory? What is the obstacle you must go over, under, or through? Our former client, Roberto Goizueta, late chairman of The Coca-Cola Company, once said: "You can't fight a war without an enemy."

In fact, defining an enemy is key to defining victory. When you print a message, you can use dark ink on a light background or light ink on a dark background, but not dark on dark or light on light. Contrast communicates.

But be careful. Unless you are actually up against Darth Vader, the unquestionable and immutable incarnation of evil, it is far better to set your campaign's focus beyond a particular opponent and laser in on a problem that your constituents all recognize, acknowledge, and can agree upon. The "enemy" must be defined as the *enemy of our mutual win*. Beat that nemesis, and you win for everybody.

After many years and many hundreds of corporate projects, we can tell you that what we hear most often from clients is, "The enemy is us." It's like they've all cut out and framed that iconic Walt Kelly comic strip in which Pogo recasts Oliver Hazard Perry's message of triumph, "We have met the enemy, and they are ours," as "We have met the enemy, and they are us." The point is that our clients are smart. By the time they call us, they have already recognized that the "enemy" is:

- ✪ *our* status quo,
- ✪ *our* bureaucracy,
- ✪ *our* heritage of being reactive, not proactive, and
- ✪ *our* willingness to allow X Dark Force Competitor to win this category.

In political elections, corporate leadership decisions, projects, and challenges, the enemy is *always* the enemy of change.

What keeps us from getting to real success, to the real win-win for us and our customers? What's the enemy of change, the obstacle to the win-win? Answer these questions clearly and personally, and you will be on the path to commanding the will, commitment, and hard work of your supporters.

Seven: This Is the Future I Want to Lead Us to

Back in the 1980 presidential contest, Jimmy Carter focused his campaign on #6 above: the enemy of our mutual win. He famously defined it in "the enemy is us" terms, describing it as a "national malaise" of droopiness and cynicism that kept America from moving forward.

And that is where the Man from Plains left it—for Ronald Reagan to pick up, shove aside, and walk beyond.

Jimmy Carter wasn't wrong to define the enemy as us. His mistake was to focus exclusively on that enemy, so that vision was all he had to offer voters. He failed to lead. More precisely, he failed to lead voters beyond the enemy he defined for them. In contrast, Ronald Reagan took voters by the hand and showed them what lay beyond the vision—not false, but myopic—of Jimmy Carter. Reagan felt the voters' pain. He defined it, however, not as a "malaise," but as "America's greatness, trying to get out," a greatness suppressed by bureaucracy, over-taxation, and a lack of true vision.

Reagan was an optimist. Fortunately for him, that optimism was in his nature, and so it was sincere and always came across as such. His best-known utterance—our favorite, certainly—could only have come from the mind of a man who felt lucky in life "America's best days are yet to come. Our proudest moments are yet to be. Our most glorious achievements are just ahead." Well, a lot of people feel lucky in life, but few of them rise to leadership. In the case of the Great Communicator, he was not only able to use his personal feeling of good fortune to overcome a hell of a lot of obstacles himself, but also to project that feeling and make it contagious. Famously, Reagan defined "that shining city on a hill" as the America we could *all* have. Twenty-five years later, Donald Trump achieved almost instant momentum with "Make America Great Again!" Will he be able to capture the truly inclusive emotion of Reagan's "*Together*, we will make America great again"? As this is being written, who knows?

We've already noted Disney chairman/CEO Bob Iger's definition of a successful corporate culture. It is achieved when each employee (in Disney's case and colloquium, each "cast member") feels, "I am a part of something great. I can make a difference. Somebody recognizes that I make a difference." That "something great" is the future of every family who goes to a Disney Park, takes a Disney cruise, or goes to a Disney movie. It is family fun, the rare mutual moments we all share and that bring us for that time closer, in spite of our divisive squabbles and chemical changes.

Bill Gates used to define the future every year at the big COMDEX show, forerunner of today's CES (Consumer Electronics Show). He would say that he was going to talk about what life will be like in ten years—and then he would add, "And I'm not going to mention the word Microsoft." Next, he would go on to describe walking into a room that instantly begins to adapt to you, your needs, and desires, creating the perfect levels of temperature, light, and humidity. The digital spaces on the walls would fill with art that makes your heart—and only *your* heart—sing. Your favorite soothing or motivating music would begin to play in the background. Your workplace would begin to order things as you need them to accomplish your own personal goals.

As promised, "Microsoft" was not mentioned. Bill didn't need to. Bill didn't need to mention that all of these miracles of indulgence would be working on a Windows platform. It was clear that *his* version of the future was a kind of operating system, a platform, and all the others at COMDEX—the competitors who hated Microsoft so much—would begin to see and feel their own place on *his* platform, in *his* future. The key for Gates? It was *his* future that *they* were thinking about now.

Bill Gates truly believed everyone will benefit from the full expression of the personal computer's potential as Microsoft enabled it. He had personally written the mission that drove Microsoft through its first decade: "A Computer on Every Desk, in Every Home."

As much as they may have disliked one another, Jobs and Gates were fellow revolutionaries, and they knew it. So were other competitors, such as Larry Ellison (Oracle), Mitch Kapor (Lotus), and Jim Manzi (Lotus). Geez Louise, Microsoft didn't even make computers, but it did make the ubiquity of the personal computer its mission in life. That was freaking brilliant, and it motivated the company's "Microserfs" (the term that became the title of Doug Coupland's terrific first novel) in an all-nighter that lasted for years.

Archimedes boasted, "Give me a lever and a place to stand, and I'll move the world." But we aren't boasting when we invite you to **Define an optimistic and personally appealing future: Give everybody a stake in that future, and they'll move the world to enable you to lead them there.**

✪ Step 7 ✪
CONTROL the Dialogue

Ramp up your communication skills to command change.

"What is **he** doing here?" Trump demanded.

There was an awkward silence. This was just the first minute of the second 2015 Republican debate. It was like Muhammad Ali starting his Bolo Punch just as the fighters were touching gloves in round one. Trickeration. The news anchors were momentarily gobsmacked.

Down at the end of fifteen Republican candidates, Senator Rand Paul was busily shuffling through his notes as if he were studying for a chem exam when this Trump two-by-four hit him upside the head. The cameras swung down toward him. He began a reflexive defense of his place at the grown-up table, but any fight fan could tell his knees *were wobbly and he was trying simply to survive the first round of a fifteen rounder, covering up and holding on for dear life.*

This, ladies and gentlemen, is called "controlling the dialogue." And it's a prime Trumpian example of what it takes to get control of the dialogue: change stuff up. Throw the slider. Hurl the monkey wrench, if you have to. Do what needs doing to change the dialogue so you can get control of the dialogue. That's rule number one of Step 7.

Every campaign is a kind of conversation, a dialogue between two or more candidates. Some call it a debate—the long debate that is the entire campaign, which includes many interactions, direct and indirect, between the candidates in addition to the set-piece network-sponsored public debates. The entire campaign can be looked upon as a debate, with the voters as an audience. Their votes decide who won the long debate.

Welcome to the Debate

Every competition in which you take part, even the quiet competitions within your own organization, will find you in a similar kind of debate. You will be compared and contrasted with other candidates by stakeholders who are evaluating your fitness to lead. This is true whether you are CEO, vying for CEO, or simply taking on a particular project or trying to guide the organization in meeting a challenge.

Successful candidates understand that the entire campaign and everything they communicate in that campaign contributes to shaping the outcome of the campaign dialogue. Everything communicates, and every detail of what you do and say will make a difference.

Competing product brands may be thought of as candidates vying in the marketplace for the most consumer votes. Their presence, packaging, associated advertising, and consumer response (often on social media) are the substance of a debate about their benefits and differentiation in every possible category. Ultimately, the subject of this debate is market value—to consumers, distributors, resellers, and many other constituents.

Within a given company and between competing companies, there is an ongoing debate as well. It may be very subtle, implicit in the differing styles and approaches of different leadership candidates. Or it may be a wide-open debate on a key issue or challenge within the company or between competitors. True, over time, the board of directors often chooses the CEO, and the CEO often chooses other C-Suite officers. But there is also a consensus of top employees and others in the company's system that puts the momentum behind one or two candidates. And the employees listen in on the debate every day in a very focused and critical way. After all, *their* careers ride on the differences between leaders.

We have seen open employee revolts against the directors' choice of leader. In union shops, one form that such a revolt may take is a strike. Even when unions are not involved, however, the internal debate can spill out to the public. This was certainly the case with BP and the 2010 Deepwater Horizon Gulf oil spill. CEO Tony Hayward famously described the monumental disaster as "relatively tiny" in comparison with "the very big ocean." That was bad enough, but when he later announced, "I'd like my life back"—by which he apparently meant getting back to England to race his (relatively) huge sailing yacht—the public call for his scalp was deafening. And it undoubtedly heaped a few billions onto the eventual $18.7 billion in fines BP was forced to pay.

Under pressure (and who isn't?), Hayward lost control of the dialogue and thereby lost the debate. In our consulting work—and in this book—we look at any contest from the perspective of "control of the dialogue," or "control of the debate." **Control of the dialogue is mastery over your opponents. It is about**

continually exploiting the leverage of effective communication to dictate action and outcome.

In sports, it's called momentum. If you are an informed football fan, you know what it means to take "control of the line of scrimmage." It is about which team takes the initiative across the no man's land between them. There is one thing besides the scoreboard to watch in order to know what *is* happening and what *will* happen in a game. Just keep your eye on those few inches of battleground at the scrimmage line. One team will seize the advantage, getting across the line of scrimmage first, hitting the other line, and putting them on their heels in defense—no matter if this team is playing offense *or* defense themselves. In the real trench warfare that is football, *this* is the most intense and interesting battle. It's why the New England Patriots will cycle eight different defensive linemen, so that they are always fresh for this fight.

Truth to tell, from a strategic and tactical point of view, it's a remarkably short step from football—the most warlike of sports—to actual war. The winning advantage typically goes to whichever side controls battlefield events and the pace of those events. Being on the attack—playing offense—is both the scariest and winningest strategy. It may feel safe to run, but, as every soldier knows, the retreat is the most difficult and dangerous of all field maneuvers. With your back to the enemy, you give up control. And it's the same in political or corporate combat. Control of the dialogue, which means staying on the attack, means control over your fate—and that of your opponent as well.

The football team that dominates the line of scrimmage wins the game. The army that dominates the battlefield wins the battle. The candidate, team, or brand that controls the debate wins the debate.

Controlling the dialogue means really and truly controlling the dialogue: controlling the issues to be debated, the timing of challenges and confrontations, the pace and nature of change in the debate, and the sense of anticipation that keeps the audience (consumers, voters) *and* the opponent tensely wondering, "What *will* she say next?"

Play Offense

The highest principle of insurgent strategy is always to play offense. First and foremost, that means seriously resolving never to play defense.

No matter how it sounds, this isn't a matter of constant aggressiveness. Recklessness takes a special kind of craziness that may succeed—very occasionally—but it has a real and more frequent downside. As General George S. Patton said, "The idea is not to die for your country. The idea is to get the other dumb son of a bitch to die for *his* country." Playing offense is most often a matter of creativity, timing, and agility—none of which is improved by recklessness. Most importantly, playing offense is not an event, a one-time deal, but is a permanent operating procedure, an ongoing hit-'em-where-they-ain't strategic orientation. It is, in short, a career strategy.

In any contest, control of the dialogue is a massive advantage. Yet it is seldom achieved through brute mass. Most often, it is the result of cunning, commitment, and strategic discipline. Agility trumps power again and again in political, business, or military contexts alike.

Change

As we noted in the Donald Trump debate approach at the beginning of this step, there is one thing that always gains control of the dialogue. It is change.

The status quo of any contest, even the opening kickoff or tipoff in sports, is the steady state of the dialogue. To gain the advantage, you must alter that state by bringing it to a new level.

Then you must maintain it there, or regain it there if lost. Gaining, maintaining, and regaining control of the dialogue is achieved by means of the same weapon: change.

Learn to love change, if you want to learn to love success in the Information Age.

Disrupt

This is today's favorite synonym for *change*. Unlike most new descriptions of simple political or market forces, we like this one. Picture this: a floor of a room with hundreds of ping pong balls lying there in perfect solitude—the steady state. Toss another ball into the room, and they begin to move. If they all move, it's a chain reaction.

What we love in politics and in business is when the molecules are in motion. That means opportunity. For the insurgent, change means opportunity. Think of each ping pong ball as a molecule and each molecule as a consumer, user, or usage occasion. When you toss in the insurgent molecule, you start the disruption, and you create opportunity precisely because the status quo has been upset. There is opportunity to win another usage or purchase decision. There is opportunity to win over another user. As advocates of insurgency, we love that. If, on the other hand, we held stock in a big-box incumbent, we'd be feeling the kind of queasy that comes when your wallet gets a little lighter.

To create the opportunity to gain control of the dialogue in a market, a campaign, a company, you must first disrupt the status quo.

The big, successful incumbent companies resist disruption the way a glassblower fights the urge to hiccup. They don't want to get burned. Our friend Bob Shapiro, a founder of the innovation company Sandbox Industries and former chairman of Monsanto, came up with a great description of the incumbent market leader's attitude toward change in a private meeting with us in Chicago recently: "At the center of the company, at its core, there is this cool, serene place where they believe their essence is kept. Yes, they may accept a little change far out on the periphery, way out in the 'burbs, far from this core. But never, ever will they allow change to get near that essence. It's a religious issue with most of them."

We recognize there is disruption and then there is *disruption*. You can disrupt the quiet dinner party with a crass joke or by dousing someone with a glass of wine. (Red works better than white for this purpose.) In much the same way, you can disrupt a market with a stunt. It's what lesser-known or desperately out-of-the-dialogue brands like Go Daddy and Cheetos have tried to do with "edgy"—to use a current term we absolutely hate—Super Bowl TV commercials.

Crude, childish stunts may intrude on someone's reverie or break someone's concentration, but actual disruption—meaningful change—is effective only if it changes the prevailing dialogue. To do this, it must be both relevant—at least to a defined set of target constituents—and different. **Only *relevant* differentiation creates value.**

You Are Not Alone

Disruption will change the dialogue in a market, but when you disrupt a market and set those molecules in motion, others will also see the opportunity. The herd instinct being what it is, most of those others will follow your lead. Someone, however, may add a new change to your change, and if that new change happens to be both more relevant and more different, that someone stands a real chance of wresting control from you.

One of the most significant market effects in American business during the past generation has been the ability of insurgents to change the dialogue in a market without provoking resistance or even reaction from the market incumbent. For instance, Coke allowed Pepsi *seven* years of the Pepsi Challenge before deigning to respond. AT&T gave MCI more than twenty years to establish itself with its "Friends & Family" value proposition. McDonald's allowed Burger King to establish its brand position against the Golden Arches for several years with its "flame-broiled versus frying" disruption of the fast-food business. The big airlines ignored upstart Southwest as it established its meaning in smaller business markets. Budweiser, Miller, and Coors (now trying to become one humongous sitting-duck incumbent), saw the march of insurgent craft beers, but didn't see the effect of that march—at least not until the market had been fundamentally changed.

Count on this: Incumbents hate change. That's the most important characteristic that separates them from insurgents. **Insurgents love change. To them, change is opportunity. Incumbents hate change. To them, change is threat.**

Change is threat. And yet incumbents seldom respond quickly or effectively to the threat. Typically, they all deal with it the same way. They ignore it, deny it, and then they react to it in a process that can take years. In those years, the marketplace will surely change. When consumers are presented with new choices, "they choose to choose," as Sergio Zyman, the famously disruptive "Ayacola" CMO of The Coca-Cola Company declared.

The thing is, once they try new choices and choose to add them to their personal menu, the market is changed. Forever.

Offer Control

So, we've been talking about how to gain control of a market or organizational dialogue. Everybody wants control. Consumers are always looking for more control. That's why they "choose to choose," seeking choice, change, customization, connection, and convenience—all the trappings of control. This is a Cliff's Notes distillation of market dialogues today. Markets today are all about who will provide the sense of control consumers crave, whether the product in question is sneakers or personal finance.

Even in markets where consumers expect change, such as technology, disruption takes the same form, follows the same process. Google changed many markets when it created the concept of online search. It was the giant ping pong ball that jolted all others. It disrupted or even eliminated the White Pages, Yellow Pages, 411, city and country guidebooks, many reference books, and the whole idea of "going into the stacks" at the university library to study for exams. By offering up new choices, what Bill Gates called "information at your fingertips," Google changed many, many other consumer or B2B markets, by opening up opportunity for insurgent brands to reach consumers. The disruption of Google allowed the disruption of many other companies to shake up other markets and categories.

Amazon's disruption of markets has been almost as sweeping. Jeff Bezos is a remarkably energetic and inventive insurgent. We haven't worked with him, but we suspect he has that same level of paranoia coursing through his veins as Jobs and Gates. Gates often repeated the old New York City adage: "Just because you're paranoid, doesn't mean they're *not* out to get you."

Bezos continues to disrupt the market leader, which now is his own company. That, in fact, is the only way you remain a market leader today. You must keep changing and refreshing your value proposition. Taking on the literally hidebound bookselling industry was a tremendous feat. Logistically, though, think of what it means to create same-day delivery of many of the items that can be bought on Amazon. And what *can't* be bought on Amazon? Bezos even achieved a breathtaking "define the future" moment on CBS's *60 Minutes*, when he had Charlie Rose's jaw dropping by demonstrating delivery via drone. Good luck flying the friendly skies if that one actually ever happens! Still, it was a PR event of seismic magnitude.

Bezos, like Steven Jobs, has made disruption a process, a way of life at Amazon. A *New York Times* piece from August 15, 2015, titled "Inside Amazon: Wrestling Big Ideas in a Bruising Workplace," suggested that Bezos's company is perpetually in the process of "conducting an experiment in how far it can push white-collar workers to get them to achieve its ever expanding ambitions." Recruits are "told to forget the 'poor habits' they learned" at other jobs, and when they "hit the wall" because of this insurgent's unrelenting pace, they are told that the only solution is to "Climb the wall." The status quo is not just an enemy at Amazon, it is a bitter enemy. Workers are encouraged to "tear apart one another's ideas in meetings," they are encouraged to adopt a 24/7 work life. Not only do e-mails often arrive after midnight, they are followed up with text messages asking why they were not answered. The company actually "boasts" that employees are held to "unreasonably high" standards. Innovation is demanded—and rewarded with bonuses in the form of stock. Fail to innovate, however, and you are culled in a process a "former Amazon human resources director" described as "purposeful Darwinism."

Never-ending disruption has produced tremendous value at Amazon and has made Bezos as well as many of his employees very wealthy. "Thanks in part to its ability to extract the most from employees," the *Times* reporters write, "Amazon is stronger than ever," with a market value of $250 billion and a CEO, Bezos, ranked by *Forbes* as the fifth-wealthiest human being on the planet. On the other hand, its relentless pace has (according to some) led to "cancer, miscarriages and other personal crises" among some workers. The *Times* writers quote one employee, who "lasted less than two years," recalling that "You walk out of a conference room and you'll see a grown man covering his face. Nearly every person I worked with, I saw cry at their desk."

The idea of upgrades, developed and defined by the software industry, established the idea that any product will constantly change to be better. At Microsoft, we established a motto: "The product is never finished." It was a novelty twenty or so years ago, but it's simply true of all tech products today. They continually change and change for the better. Consumers anticipate that market disruption. Conditioned by market insurgents, consumers love change, and woe betide the tech product that doesn't accept that reality.

There is no cruise control in technology today (or anywhere else, for that matter). The market rules are written on a white board in wipe-away Sharpie. That's been the case in the 2016 presidential campaign. Traditional rules have been smeared right off the board by voter anger, alienation, and cynicism. And it's no different in every consumer market, where the frustration of shoppers is always answered by change. Change is a new product or service. Change is a new craft beer. It's Uber, and it's Airbnb. New ideas get traction with consumers faster than ever, with more and more of them acting like early adopters, confident about trying the newest new thing.

Change and disruption have to be a way of life, a part of your company culture, and your own identity. If you don't like it, go into academia, which may be the last bastion of the status quo or, at least, the last place in which change unfolds at the pace of a glacier—which used to be really, really slow, at least before we heard about global warming. In any case, change in the academy is a lot slower than the hopping hot frying pan effect that rules other industries, markets, and aspects of our culture. Just watch Amazon continue to change and change again. Amazon keeps the market molecules in motion. In theory, that creates opportunity for others as well, but it's like going for a jump ball against Kareem Abdul-Jabbar. Change and disruption get the ball every time.

Another of the great disrupters of the past decade has been Red Bull Energy Drink. We've extolled them before for their Wee Willie Winkie "hit 'em where they ain't" success. It's what Hall of Fame NFL coach Vince Lombardi used to call "running to daylight." When they couldn't get a deal for distribution by the powerful incumbent distribution networks of Coke or Pepsi bottlers, they went to beer distributing companies. That already declining market offered space for a new product and a new revenue stream. Good as this was, it created the problem of being delivered to a lot of liquor stores and convenience stores instead of the supermarkets that are the keystone of Coke's and Pepsi's distribution strategy. Red Bull managed to find daylight by deciding to position the beverage as a mixer with alcohol, thereby enabling young folks to "boogie all night," as is their wont. In addition, Red Bull handed out free cases of their product to bouncers and bartenders, who had to stay sharp all night as their customers were a-boogie-ing. These marketing decisions anointed Red Bull with an urban legend brand position as something slightly dangerous and a little illicit.

In convenience stores, Red Bull placed the product near the cash register, not in the soft drink cooler. "I think I'll have a soft drink" is a commodity decision, whereas "I think I could use some energy" is a differentiator that reinforced their relevance—you can feel the energy!—and distinction from Coke and Pepsi. Moreover, since Red Bull couldn't do the usual big, established sports endorsements and sponsorships—Pepsi and Coke cockblocked them there—they started inventing their own sports: X-Games, extreme sailing, extreme gaming, the world's highest parachute jump (broadcast live), and on and on. The running of Red Bulls means running for daylight all the way.

Dictate the Issues for Debate

When you do gain control of a market dialogue or the leadership dialogue in your company, you control the issues to be debated. Again, we remind you that being spontaneous doesn't mean being impulsive or reckless. Map out the issues. As candidate Trump reminded the press again and again during the 2015-2016 primary season, nobody was talking about immigration until he called it out in the year's first Republican debate. Once you have control of the dialogue, you must be proactive, never reactive. To be sure, you may respond to public or company events, but you have to recognize that everyone else will do the same. Getting ahead of events is always best. Control the debate? No. *Dictate* the debate.

Develop a winning game plan long before the game begins. Trial lawyers live or die by the commandment, Thou shalt not ask a witness any question to which you don't already have the answer. The same is true in the campaign debate. Never guess at the answer to the market questions. Don't assume the answers. Don't jump in with common—ugh!—sense. Find the answers so you'll know in advance.

As far as laying out the issues, rely on your 3x5 card messages as an outline. The debate you're in is about defining the stakes in your election: in the issues you raise and in the win-win for you and the stakeholders you need to engage. The headline of your 3x5 card should answer the question, "What is this campaign all about?"

If it's all about you, chances are it won't succeed. It has to be all about those who will decide the outcome. They are the key stakeholders of your campaign, including the board of directors, your peers, other employees, major suppliers, market partners, trade and business media, distributors and retailers, as well as your customers and consumers. Focus upon them by the issues you articulate. Focus on them the way you communicate to them.

It is possible that someone may wrest the initiative from you at some point and gain control of the dialogue. That sucks, but at least it makes your next assignment eminently clear. Work like hell to win back control. The only way to do this is to change the dialogue. So you'd better be ready for that, too.

The object of the game, though, is not to cede control of the dialogue and to constantly lead the debate. This is done primarily via the substance of your messages. So outline the four or five key issues from your 3x5 card messages you will use in every way possible to define your campaign. For instance:

✪ We need to change from our status quo approach to our marketplace. The marketplace has changed, but we haven't.

✪ We must create a much quicker drumbeat of new ideas into the market.

✪ We must develop an off-campus, out-of-our-comfort zone ability to work with true insurgents and inventors.

✪ We need more diversity—not just more diverse individuals, but also diverse ideas, opinions, and approaches. That will create a change-friendly environment, and that's what we need.

Outline the issues. Lay them out like the Xs and Os of a Bill Belichick game plan: first we do this, then this, then this. No huddle. You must have the substance of the campaign defined in advance. Relevant and different substance is always important.

And then there's timing. It's important, too.

Timing

While the market or your company is beginning to react to the first change in the dialogue—after trying to ignore or deny it—you need to introduce the second one. That is how you keep up the pace of change. Just when it's dawning on your competition that your first or second idea is gaining traction, you are introducing the third.

This is the way Mickey Drexler forever changed the pace of retail merchandising when he was running Gap. His main competition back then was the big mall anchor department stores. Their pace of change was "back to school" … "holiday" … "spring fashions" … "summer" … "back to school." Of course, interspersed were sales events resulting from the failure to sell out any of those regular events. Too slow. Too dull. So Mickey began changing the merchandising of the Gap stores on a *weekly* basis. He was constantly changing things up. Nothing radical, mind you: it was still flannel and logo T-shirts and khakis for men and simple casual fashion for women. But to the young person walking through the mall, the Gap window and wide doorway always provided welcome distraction—and that rhymes with disruption. It was the disruption that repeatedly pulled customers away from the big department stores. By the time Mickey left Gap for J. Crew, the industry had accepted his pace of change, and the big guys were vast, empty warehouses of retail despair.

Anticipation/Tension

When you maintain control of the dialogue through continual disruption, you create an important quality for your brand, something beyond the basics of presence/awareness, relevance, differentiation, credibility, and imagery. It is anticipation, as in: **"What *will* they think of next?"**

Long after the untimely passing of Steven Jobs, Apple still has this brand quality. It is a remarkable thing. It creates a "watch this space" aura around your brand—product brand or personal brand. It engages the audience to look beyond you in the here and now to anticipate the future you. Generally, it is a deliciously positive anticipation—though it is also true that the likes of the incumbent cable TV company and the major airlines create nothing but negative anticipation. It wasn't "What *will* they think of next?" but "What *now?*" or "*Now* what?" Certainly as well, many politicians and most American voters feel the negative anticipation projected by both major political parties: "Here we go again." But if you can engage your audience of constituents or stakeholders in a process of positive disruption, they will always look to you first for the next new thing. And *that*, friends, is gold.

The Art of Disruption

The recent history of presidential debates in the United States has provided many lessons in the art of disruption. It comes in the verbal form of agility, the quick and cutting remark, the spontaneous rejoinder that is seldom truly spontaneous. Political leaders polish and prepare their turns of phrase in the hope they will get a chance to use them. You may remember some of these:

- ✪ Ronald Reagan, debating President Jimmy Carter in 1980: "Ask yourself, 'Are you better off now than you were four years ago? Is it easier for you to go and buy things in the stores than it was four years ago? Is there more or less unemployment in the country than there was four years ago? Is America as respected throughout the world as it was?"

- ✪ Vice President Walter Mondale, debating Senator Gary Hart in 1984: "When I hear your new ideas, I'm reminded of that ad, 'Where's the beef?'"

✪ Later that year, Ronald Reagan debated candidate Mondale, even as some were grumbling that Reagan, age seventy-three, was too old to run for reelection. After Mondale declared himself above such ageism, Reagan announced, "I want you to know also I will not make age an issue of this campaign. I am not going to exploit for political purposes my opponent's youth and inexperience."

The 1988 campaign had a few beauties, too. For instance, in the vice presidential debate, Democratic Senator Lloyd Bentsen was pitted against Republican Dan Quayle, who less than wisely compared his youthfulness to that of JFK:

Quayle: "I have as much experience in the Congress as Jack Kennedy did when he sought the presidency."

Bentsen: "I knew Jack Kennedy; Jack Kennedy was a friend of mine. (*beat*) Senator, you're no Jack Kennedy."

In the Democratic presidential debates that year, Bernard Shaw of CNN began with an incendiary question for Michael Dukakis. "Governor, if Kitty Dukakis were raped and murdered, would you favor an irrevocable death penalty for the killer?"

Dukakis' answer was dry and bloodless as a stone. "No, I don't, Bernard. And I think you know that I've opposed the death penalty during all of my life. I don't see any evidence that it's a deterrent, and I think there are better and more effective ways to deal with violent crime."

Governor Mario Cuomo, asked the same question about the rape and murder of his own wife, said, "I would get a baseball bat. I would search that murderer out. And I would hope that someone would find me and stop me before I beat that person to death."

Although Dukakis won the nomination, he was mortally wounded from that moment on, as he took on George H. W. Bush, and, more importantly, Roger Ailes, Bush's campaign manager.

"Sorry, oops!" was the unforgettable and irreversible comment of Governor Rick Perry in the 2012 Republican debates. He announced that, as president, he would immediately eliminate three government agencies, listed two, then stumbled and confessed he could not remember the third. And although Perry withdrew from the 2016 presidential race, he got in a pretty deft left hook against Donald Trump: "We don't need an apprentice in the White House. We've got one right now."

These may seem to be little more than off-the-cuff witticisms, but what they really are is utterances designed to usurp control of the dialogue and disrupt the opponent's line of argument and persuasion. They push the audience off the path along which the other candidate has been leading them. In developing your own messaging, think about how you might prepare similar opportunistic responses to likely competitive reactions or criticism. Counter-punching works in business and politics as well as it does in boxing. It sounds spontaneous, which means that it seems like a revelation of reality itself. If you want to orchestrate reality—and that is what winners do—rehearse spontaneity. The harder you rehearse the opportunistic, the more spontaneous it will seem.

✪ Step 8 ✪
GAIN Momentum

Keep doing the doable and moving the movable, push the offense forward, reach deep, find another gear, surge.

Big Mo, positive momentum, is unquestionably the most powerful drug, licit or illicit, known to humankind. It activates adrenaline, unleashes endorphins, heightens every sense, and sharpens every instinct. It makes a winning team or organization absolutely unstoppable. Performance-enhancing snake oil has been around forever, but Big Mo—it's the real thing. It's the great-granddaddy of the real thing.

There is no yin without its yang, and you have to understand that momentum comes in two varieties, positive and negative. Unfortunately, negative momentum is nearly as potent as Big Mo.

159

It's just that it works in reverse. It saps a team or a company of strength, cunning, and agility. It's Kryptonite.

Seizing and maintaining positive versus negative momentum is the difference between a winning and losing campaign.

Negative Momentum: Again, the 1988 Dukakis for President campaign is widely considered the classic example of the baleful effect of negative momentum. Are you old enough to remember the video of Mike Dukakis riding in a tank and wearing both a ludicrously outsized helmet and an abashed yet shit-eating grin? (If not, you're certainly young enough to find it on YouTube.) This image was the archetypal product of a campaign team dubbed The Gang That Couldn't Shoot Straight. That, in fact, was an excessively generous assessment. They were shooting blanks. They came out of the Democratic National Convention with loads of Big Mo, only to allow it to drain away and turn negative as the campaign wore on and Roger Ailes counseled George H. W. Bush in the art of taking and then maintaining control of the dialogue.

Positive Momentum: The 1992 Clinton for President Campaign, with that "It's the economy, stupid" focus, is universally considered a classic example of discipline, creativity, and forward drive. With Big Mo at their backs, the Clintonites blew out incumbent President George H. W. Bush, who had blown out Dukakis in the last election.

As discussed previously, a fascinating fact about these contrasting campaigns is that they were run by pretty much the same team, the same political people. The results they produced could not have been more different. We mean it, *could not have been.* Dukakis lost. Clinton won. This proves the central importance of leadership in creating positive momentum—or negative momentum. As Dukakis infamously said of the Reagan administration, translating an old Greek expression, "The fish rots from the head down." Leaders lead. They create momentum—adrenalin-pumping positive or fish-head-rotting negative momentum.

Leaders lead. Leaders create momentum. They create it by taking, maintaining, or retaking control of the campaign dialogue for month after month in the much-too-long American electoral process.

It's rarely pedal-to-the-metal from announcement to Election Day. Rare indeed is the campaign that can get along without a few pit stops along the way. Almost all campaigns are a series of separate events, each presenting the possibility of acceleration, deceleration, or a slam into reverse. Most of the time, a talented leader takes the opportunity to accelerate by winning control of the dialogue, maintaining it, or getting it back. They lead a campaign in a continual effort to keep moving forward as fast as possible.

Hillary Clinton had momentum early in her 2008 campaign. In fact, her election was widely considered "inevitable." But her campaign made a critical strategic mistake that stalled her effort and handed an opening to the almost unknown first-term Senator Barack Obama. Her campaign strategist, Mark Penn, looked at the same research everyone else in politics had seen that year. It showed that the American people wanted fundamental change in Washington. Penn chose instead to position Clinton based on her vast government experience. Not unreasonable. After all, what could be wrong about having experience—*vast* experience? What could be—and was—wrong was the fact that the voters were telling everybody who would listen that they wanted change. Clinton grabbed experience, leaving the Barack Obama campaign to own change. Sure, *he* would be the first African American president. But *she* would have been the first woman president. She could have played the change card just as legitimately and effectively as Team Obama did. Was Hillary Clinton the victim of bad advice? Well, remember, the candidate is CEO of the campaign. It was Penn's mistake, but CEO Hillary owned it.

Some campaigns lose momentum and then gain it back. That's happened in many presidential campaign cycles. Candidates have been written off, only to come back like gangbusters. That's why Bill Clinton was called "The Comeback Kid."

In business, the same laws of motion apply. The leadership campaign must use projects, competitive initiatives, challenges, and crises as opportunities to gain and accelerate momentum. There will be lulls and there will be competitive thrusts, but, as in politics, the leader must take as many opportunities as possible to impart a sense of momentum. Take your foot off the accelerator in business, and you lose ground, which is ground you must somehow make up. That means doing whatever it takes to regain momentum.

Momentum is magical. Like all magic, the goal in performing it is to make it look easy, natural, and inevitable. That takes hard work and continual practice.

Do the Doable

As previewed in Step 1, "do the doable" is not only the foundational concept of insurgent campaigns, it is the most viable way to gain that positive momentum for your campaign.

"Do the doable" means, first of all, marshaling resources to use on the most important issues. Waste not. You want to create a culture that feels lean. Arthur Conan Doyle's Sherlock Holmes would fast for days at a time—and long before dieting was fashionable, but merely considered eccentric. His reason: "Deprivation makes the senses keener."

You want your team to feel lean and mean. Make sure they always begin with the principle of doing more with less. Hate waste, and make your people hate waste. The worst waste is the kind that is taken for granted in most organizations, the constant drip, drip, drip of stupid waste. It's the kind of thing that is accepted by everyone, until an accountant with a sharp pencil in the employ of an activist investor begins to add it up and make a case against incompetent management.

When hackers break into the accounts of the big banks, they don't try to pull off a big-time Willie Sutton–like heist all at once. Instead, they spend a month or so in there establishing the constant drip, drip, drip cadence of stealing a little at a time, often undetected, or not detected until it is way too late. The security systems at the big banks seem to consider a few million dollars chump change.

Second, "do the doable" means never aiming at the impossible or even the highly improbable goal. As the ads say, "Hope is not a strategy." What some corporations and their management consultants call "stretch goals," which are seen as virtuous *ad astra per aspera* aspirations, often backfire. Instead of instilling into employees energy and focus, they may diminish and degrade these critical qualities. When a leader sets an unreachable goal, failure to reach it can demoralize the organization and embolden and energize the competition. As the old comic line goes, "They said it couldn't be done … and it couldn't."

It's certainly the same in war, particularly when politicians, not the warriors, set the goals. And it's the same in an internal competition. Don't overreach. Don't over-promise.

As we described in Step 4, the strategic mandate behind the "do the doable" principle is to do whatever it takes to give your people a feeling of momentum. Momentum builds more momentum. So you are best off starting with very, very simple goals. Pick up the fruit that is on the ground before you even think about going for the low-hanging produce.

We apologize for yet another football analogy, but (a) sports analogies come naturally in considering any competitive situation, and (b) the two of us are broken-down ex-jocks. Besides, it was Vince Lombardi who said, "Never apologize." Or, at least, he should have. So here goes yet another: Legendary Ohio State coach Woody Hayes was famous for his running game–based strategic philosophy. He called it, "Four yards and a cloud of dust." In fact, he hated throwing passes, and also said, "Only three things can happen when you throw a pass, and two of them are bad."

That "four yards and a cloud of dust" concept is a great way to think of starting momentum on a project or against any challenge in business. Don't start out throwing that Hail Mary pass. Just make some forward progress. Just keep moving the ball down the field. Each time you gain yardage, you gain momentum, and your team gains energy and resolve. The next four yards get easier and easier.

The objective in setting objectives is to keep them simple, keep them attainable, and keep them in clear sight of your team. **Forget long-term planning. That's for management consultants. You want and need immediate momentum.** Besides, creating momentum is the only way you're going to reach your long-term goals.

Set modest goals with modest expectations. Then celebrate every win as you win it. Celebrate modestly at first. Forget the plastic participation trophies, and bring forth heartfelt recognition and appreciation of every success along the way toward your ultimate goals. You will create a greater sense of accomplishment among your employees and those who judge your accomplishments by defining goals modestly and then over-delivering on them.

A caveat: The modesty over your do-the-doable goals should not keep you from defining ultimate success as a Great Thing and a Better World for all stakeholders. Make sure you link every objective and every immediate success as mile markers on the road to Something Great. Just keep all eyes on the *next* mile marker, the one just up ahead.

In defining the destination of your efforts as a great and noble goal that is a big win for all stakeholders, involve the people on your team and in your organization as participants in planning the ultimate destination. *This is where we're all going together!*

Involving them also lets you give them ownership of the results and the extra effort it will take to deliver those results. This, in turn, will also give them ownership of the strategy that is a road map to reach the great destination that you yourself have defined. And as you develop each objective and each strategy to reach that great destination, involve your people. They will much more readily take responsibility for results if they take ownership of setting the goals that motivate success. Collaboration creates an energy all its own.

Track Progress Day-to-Day

As we write this, the People's Republic of China's Communist Party bigwigs met recently to develop their thirtieth Five Year Plan. (If you're doing the math, you've already figured out that in the 67-year history of the PRC, they've abandoned more than a few of those five-year plans well before the five years were up.) To save your having to read this latest edition, the plot goes like this: The Party does whatever it takes to stay in power.

Only the Chinese bureaucracy and a few other totalitarians and marketplace incumbents can afford to continue to do long-term planning. That's because they fervently believe that their key goal—that is, survival—will last at least that long. As we've said, you have to plan for the changes coming—hopefully, because *you* are making them—tomorrow, not five years from tomorrow. Tracking progress day-to-day is important in creating and reinforcing the perception, within your organization, that daily actions lead to results. Remember the simple agenda of Mike Roberts and Frank Vizcarra in leading McDonald's out of the wilderness:

✪ What are we doing wrong?

✪ What are we doing right?

✪ What are we doing next?

Way back then, in the early 2000s, it was possible to plan sixty days ahead. Today, that time scale is a leisurely luxury.

Keep your team's eyes on today's and tomorrow's results. Keep them focused and moving forward. Celebrate small moves in the right direction. It is daily progress and, eventually, the momentum it creates that provide not only the subject for the best pep talk, but the pep talk itself. After a few days of progress, you won't even have to remind your team to "give me ONE MORE!"

Our friend Pat Mulhearn, of the disruptive new smartphone tech company MSS (Mobile Search Security), is a product of politics and recently sent us a great idea for any candidate for president: Promise the country will make progress toward paying down the multitrillion-dollar debt every day. *Every day!* Voters, employees, and consumers like to know things are *moving* in the right direction. One of the key research reporting areas of pollsters like Gallup or Rasmussen is "right track/wrong track." It is a way to show the people every day that the country is on the right track—or the wrong.

Make sure your team knows that the daily work they do is not make-work, but work that makes shit happen. By the way, never confuse this with "shit happens"—the motto of incumbency. At Core Strategy Group, our unofficial corporate motto is *Creo Merda Accidet.* And in case you don't speak Latin, the translation is "Make Shit Happen."

Take What They Give You

In most markets, the fruit on the ground is usually left there by incumbent market leaders, who have failed to pick it up, mostly because they just don't think it's important. For one reason or another, they long ago decided to eschew certain products, value propositions, geographic areas, or demographic groups. Doubtless, they had some internal rationale for the neglect back whenever they made the decision. Today, those rationales appear to be what they are: totally irrational. But the incumbents rarely take a new look.

Pepsi and Coke were afraid that regulators would feel they had crossed a line—to which they had already cozied up with caffeine and sugar—if they introduced energy drinks. So they didn't try. Oops! There went a multibillion-dollar opportunity that Red Bull, 5 Hour Energy, and others jumped on while the regulators sat still. (Maybe they needed an energy shot.)

White shoe incumbent investment banks rejected the idea of creating markets for junk bonds, because they were unseemly. "Junk is for Jews," was their executive men's room explanation. Then a Jewish guy name Michael Milken took them up on that offer. He didn't invent, but he did popularize and widely commercialize the idea of what *he* called "high yield bonds." His energy and inventiveness democratized corporate capital. It catalyzed an explosion of entrepreneurship and invention. It shook up markets. And today, no matter what they are called, all investment banks have huge high-yield bond departments.

When Henry Ford II was still CEO of the Ford Motor Company, he looked out over the company parking lot filled with the likes of the Gran Torino, Lincoln Continental, and Mercury Marquis and contentedly prophesied, "American will never drive small cars!" Welcome to America, Toyota, Nissan, Honda, Mazda, Kia, and Hyundai.

The list goes on and on. For every Uber, Airbnb, and Snapchat, there is an opportunity the big guys dissed, missed, or never even remotely imagined. Insurgents, on the other hand, run to daylight—and they've learned to count on the incumbents to leave plenty of daylight to run to.

Encourage your team to identify open opportunities in the marketplace, particularly those your own company may have always ignored for one reason or another. Maybe you've redlined certain geographic or demographic areas. Maybe you've stuck with distribution or supply chain practices about to be outmoded by new technology or new thinking. Maybe you've just been asleep at the wheel of your Crown Vic.

If you are a market leader, chances are your company's heritage and market superstitions have created and will continue to create opportunities for insurgents. That's why you should build special teams to devote themselves to beating you in the marketplace by beating you to the next new idea. That's a great way to shake up your own thinking. Attack it!

Set up your insurgent teams where they belong: off campus. We call it Outhouse Innovation. Don't be afraid of offending them. Don't be afraid that they'll think you're branding them as exiles. Putting your dedicated innovators on the periphery ensures they won't be cowed (or swayed) by the prevailing company culture. An even better idea might be to call Bob Shapiro, Nick Rosa, and Steve Engleberg at Sandbox Industries to find the two kids in a garage, wherever they are in the world, who are already devoted to the proposition of putting you out of business.

If you are an insurgent, take what they give you. Keep taking it and taking it until the incumbents move to shut out that daylight. There's a good chance that they never do. But, be assured, if they do and when they do, they will uncover yet more opportunities for you. Play offense. As an insurgent, you are in a position to analyze opportunity not just by looking at the state of the market, but also by watching what the market-leading incumbents do and fail to do. Their moves or lack of motion, together with their corporate statements defending either what they are doing or failing to do, tend to reveal the next ray of opportunity for new ideas and for new entrepreneurs.

The Open-Development Platform

To find opportunity and make continual progress against lazy incumbents, you will need a constant flow of new and disruptive ideas. That means creating what Alex Gorsky, CEO of Johnson & Johnson, calls "an innovation-friendly environment." In the high-tech world, the concept of the open-development platform means freely providing source code to any and all developers in order to encourage widespread invention and development on your platform. The most familiar example of this is Apple's open-development platform for iPhone apps—of which, according to CEO Tim Cook in October 2013, there are more than a million available.

By transferring ownership of your strategies to your team, you begin to open development. Everybody gets an ownership stake.

Creating an open-development environment is mostly a matter of your attitude toward change and disruption. **If *your company* is going to be innovation-friendly, *you* must be change-friendly.** That means you, the leader, must be open to the wild ideas, the ones that make you feel prickly heat on the back of your neck. The person behind that wild idea will likely turn up that prickly heat from time to time, and you've got to be okay with that. This means that your devotion to diversity cannot be modeled on any species of check-the-box corporate citizenship. It must instead be driven by the need to get diverse ideas, opinions, and arguments. This, in turn, requires a diverse team. Don't just talk collaboration. Make it happen on your team by setting transfer-of-ownership objectives, destinations, and strategies. You cannot choose your fellow revolutionaries by their look or pedigree, but understand that the entrepreneur class is generally dominated by mutts.

Develop a Sense of Urgency

Continually reiterate the proposition that work leads to results. In most big companies, most employees truly don't believe this. What they truly believe is that their individual efforts don't really make much of a difference. We've already noted Gallup's monitoring of "employee engagement," which shows it hovering these days around the 30% level. Thirty percent are engaged because they believe they can make a difference. The remaining 70% are convinced their efforts amount to little or nothing.

No wonder our economy remains in the downward-leaning doldrums. A lack of political leadership at every level has undoubtedly helped create this negativity, but it is the lack of leadership in the corporate sector that has done a bang-up job of compounding the problem of employee detachment. Make no mistake, these 70% of employees fear for their jobs, not because they are lazy, but because they feel their jobs are meaningless. Unfortunately, many of these employees are right. They are not deluded, and it is not their fault. The fault is in faulty leadership.

In big companies, people don't think their efforts are going to change anything.

In insurgent companies, and in most start-ups, people think they are going to change the world today and thereby own a changed future.

Where would you rather work? **As a leader of a big or small company you can create a world-changing environment or a nothing-changes environment.** The choice is yours. Dedicate *every day* to solving the same equation: *work = results*. Solving this *every day* is what makes the difference between a world-changing environment and a nothing-changes environment. An unsolved equation is called a problem. Create a sense of urgency about solving it today.

The innate sense that "everything matters" is what urgently compels entrepreneurs like Elon Musk long after they've made their first billion. Sometimes this urgency is the product of fear and paranoia. We've certainly seen a lot of that haunting the corridors of the Tech Hall of Fame. But "everything matters" can also be a source of great joy and a sense of freedom from drudgery—and this source of joy and freedom beats fear and paranoia every time. Still, even paranoia is preferable to complacency.

Eons ago, when we began Core Strategy Group, our friends in big corporations all told us the same thing: "I'd love to do what you're doing, but I couldn't stand the lack of security." It turns out that frame of reference is everything. From our viewpoint, as "freelance" consultants to a lot of big corporations, we strongly preferred the control we enjoyed over our own job security to enduring the whimsical downsizings, rightsizings, realignments, and reorganizations that give the corporate worker all the security an ant enjoys under the shadow of a rhino's impending foot. The centuries-old poignancy of the fate of the population of Pompeii is the thought of how secure these residents of a pleasant, prosperous Roman province must have felt in the benevolent shadow of Vesuvius.

Communicate urgency in everything you do and say as a leader. Say and show that details make a difference. Recognize and reward those actions and those people who do the same. Recognize and reward details.

Profligate waste is expected in big corporations, which ascribe it to a "rounding error." But insurgent teams hate waste, scorning it as a symptom of incumbent sloth and incumbent incompetence. Incumbent organizations long ago learned to live with waste as a hoarder learns to live in a pile of accumulated crap. Insurgents hate waste and hound it out.

Bernie Marcus cofounded The Home Depot and became fabulously wealthy. Successful as he was, he never stopped stalking the aisles of his stores and the lanes of his parking lots, always accosting customers in search of their pain points. He still tells the story of how he encountered a contractor with a pick-up bed loaded with lumber. Bernie gazed at the truck bed curiously.

"Why no nails in there with your lumber?" Bernie asked.

"Their nails are crap," the guy said. "They bend. I get my lumber here, and my nails at the hardware store."

You can guess what Bernie Marcus did next. He began obsessing over nails, and you can bet Home Depot's head hardware merchandiser did, too—once Bernie had a little talk with him.

Every great leader we've worked for in our professional lives demonstrated to us that they thought longer and harder about problems than we did. And *we* do think about them long and hard.

If you've ever had the privilege and the challenge of working for a great leader, you have surely gotten more than your share of 2 a.m. e-mails. They don't send them to intimidate others. They just make it a habit of believing that they can push the ball forward 24/7. Don't confuse this level of urgency with OCD. Obsessive bosses keep ungodly hours, too, but they devote them to counting paper clips. And, yes, we all have to work out our own work/life balance.

Nevertheless, err on the side of urgency. You want to balance life and work? Then err on the side of urgency in life as well as in work. Give 100% to work. Give 100% to your family. As Hall of Famer Satchel Paige said, "Don't look back. Something might be gaining on you." And in this spirit, we say, "It's useful to believe that your current or future competitors are thinking while you're sleeping … because it's often true."

Surge

Though we want you to hate waste, we also want you to know when you have to put chips on the table. For instance, we've always argued against the traditional corporate brand-awareness ad campaigns. Those campaigns guarantee long-term cash flow to advertising agencies, but don't move consumers. They are information wallpaper. They join the marketplace noise that consumers welcome the way they would tinnitus. They ignore it. If they can. If they can't, it just sort of drives them crazy, and that awareness ad campaign becomes another drop in the drip, drip, drips of stupid corporate waste.

Nevertheless, we do argue for a surge in spending around a big idea or event. Bet big on big ideas.

We take the term *surge* from David Petraeus, a brilliant general and the only successful military leader on the side of the good guys in the Iraq War. In 2007, with AQI (al Qaida in Iraq) on the move in Anbar Province and launching attack after attack in Baghdad, Petraeus led a transcendent change of U.S. strategy. It was a change of the dialogue in that war from a kind of strategic retreat encouraged by Washington political pressure to an aggressive effort that combined fighting with greater force and winning the support of Sunni Iraqis locally. Part of the surge in Iraq was an operation called "The Awakening," which encouraged the local Iraqis to take on the al Qaida "foreign fighters." *The surge* came to mean piling on more resources in a shorter timeframe: a compression that yielded the first real success for the United States since the invasion of 2003. It is success that has since been abandoned by the political class.

An example of the surge we often cite involves compressing resources into a short span of time as the basic strategy of motion picture companies when they launch a new movie. Working backward from the premiere, which is their Election Day, they devote as many resources as they can afford to a short pre-launch ramp-up. They pile specially developed movie trailers on top of ad campaigns, on top of product-placement deals and co-branding promotions, on top of interviews—even if that takes sending a star to rehab. While (as we said) the most important and determining factor in the movie's success is the quality of the picture itself, these surge campaigns often achieve liftoff of the brand idea. At the very least, we all end up remembering the title of a movie we decided not to see.

The surge is a spike that you drive through the marketplace information wallpaper and a bugle call you blow through the general marketing noise. It's Big Casino time, and it had better be supporting a relevant and different product or brand development. You want your results to be remembered, not just your marketing campaign.

Celebrate

Winning teams celebrate small successes on the way to victory. It's a way of showing mutual respect and mutual support. That's what you should do in your organization.

When we were working with Microsoft during the era of its heady 1980s successes, we'd spend a lot of time trying to find our way through the X-shaped buildings of their Redmond, Washington, campus. As we wandered down each hallway and turned each corner, we would run into another small team celebrating a new product launch or established product success. We walked under banners, through confetti, and were handed coffee mugs with the new product logo on the side. In *Microserfs,* Doug Coupland may have captured the grind-grind-grind company culture of the 1990s, but in the previous decade there was a lot of shouting and a lot of goose bumps.

Recognize the little things that mean lots in creating team momentum. Don't hesitate to criticize mistakes of omission, but occasionally reward mistakes of commission and over-zealous effort. Never celebrate participation. Always celebrate achievement, no matter how small. Celebrate. A team loves what winning feels like. It feels sweet. You want your team to have that feeling. Give it to them by doing the doable, by moving the movable, by pushing forward with each step, by reaching deep, by finding another gear, and by surging to victory. As they say in Beaverton, "Just Do It."

✪ Step 9 ✪
EXPLOIT Crisis

Plan ahead to transform crisis into yet another campaign opportunity—it's where you win or lose. Map the battlefield at regular intervals, plot scenarios, map opportunities and threats.

"I want my life back." That was the complaint of Tony Hayward, CEO of BP during the Deepwater Horizon oil spill. Given the fact that eleven men were killed in the initial explosion and fire, and that the wellhead blowout spewed 210 million gallons of oil across 2,500 to 68,000 square miles over six months, this turned out to be an unsurprisingly weak strategy for garnering public sympathy. I mean, this was the same guy who appeared on any number of live video feeds, day after day, to deliver the news that his company's well was

still spewing the sludge of death along a Gulf Coast that depended on marine life and tourism for its livelihood. For many business people and residents here, a way of life and a means of living were already smothered under tar balls. For Mr. Hayward, "getting his life back" seemed to mean going back home to racing his yacht in the pristine waters off coastal England.

At least, it must have seemed that way to the BP board of directors, who, shortly after his complaint, sent him on a permanent vacation.

Let's begin with a moment of sober, objective reflection. Crises suck.

At the very least, they disrupt corporate operations as well as the lives of their managers, employees, and shareholders. Crises give boards of directors St. Vitus's Dance because they destroy share value and shareholder confidence. The effects ripple outwards. Anybody want to bid on a slightly used VW diesel?

Okay, glad to get that warning label out of the way.

Crises suck.

Yet when *we* hear "crisis," the tips of our fingers start to tingle. Maybe we're adrenaline junkies. When the crisis hits, when doors on the executive floor start slamming shut, when muffled shouting echoes dully in the hallways, when the chief counsel starts getting night sweats, when rumors are flying like bats out of a Mexican cave at midnight, *that* is when *our* heart rates go down, when *our* minds clear.

Crisis. It's what psychologists call *our* "safe place," that place in the mind a person goes to when things get really, really tense. For most people, the "safe place" is a peaceful, sunny garden path. For us, it's the crisis war room, with cold, half-filled coffee cups and half-eaten leaden sandwiches.

We love crises. Churchill said, "Nothing clears the mind like knowing you are to be shot at dawn." And he wrote that back in the Great Boer War, when he had been captured and was scheduled to be shot at dawn. Shot dead. For real.

For us, crisis clarifies thinking. Not just ours. Most often and more important, it sharpens the clients' attention and focus. Crisis promotes what we call "pattern recognition" and PR firms that bill themselves as "Crisis Management" specialists call it (far more dramatically) "Triage." Crisis forces priorities to work their way toward the front of our minds. For thirty-some years, we've been meeting, unraveling, and exploiting business crises of every size, shape, and odor. There have been crises of challenge and crises of opportunity—though, as you are about to see, we believe *all* crises are crises of opportunity. There have been competitive crises, legal crises, and product crises. Before Symantec—which we'll get to in a minute—there was Microsoft under siege by the DOJ and the determined prosecuting attorney Joel Klein. There was Steven Jobs being fired by John Sculley, whom he himself had hired away from PepsiCo to manage the company and generally be "the grown-up in the room." There was New Coke, maybe the biggest crisis-to-opportunity turnaround in history. There was United States Attorney Rudy Giuliani against Wall Street's Mike Milken. There were a couple of actions Ted Turner hurled against Rupert Murdoch. There was Gerry Hsu of Avanti Corporation pleading no-contest to charges of intellectual property theft. There was Verizon's post-9/11 actions to move beyond the destruction of its downtown building and get the New York Stock Exchange back up and running in six days. There were the untimely and tragic deaths of two McDonald's CEOs in succession, leading to the unlikely rise of Mike Roberts as quite possibly the most successful CEO in McDonald's history. There are several other examples we're still not allowed to mention.

What we *can* mention is a call that came to us from Jon Lazarus one day. Jon was Bill Gates's get-things-done man. He was a no-joke guy. We'd never even seen him crack a smile. When he called, the hair stood up on the back of your neck.

"I have a question for you."

Uh-oh.

"Would you work for a competitor of ours?" Jon asked.

Ah-hah! We thought it was a trick question, a test of our loyalty to Microsoft.

"Well, no, Jon. Of course not."

"No, no, no!" he said impatiently. "*Would* you? Would you be willing to? It's a sort of competitor who's actually been a good friend. See? He needs help. Bill would appreciate it if you'd help him."

And, so it was *Yes, sir! Whatever we can do, sir!*

The "sort of" competitor was Gordon Eubanks, then-CEO of Symantec, now retired. Symantec was (and still is) best known as a company that makes lots of antivirus and other security software—bestselling stuff. At the time, Microsoft included its own antivirus protection bundled into Windows. In the midst of the assault on Microsoft by the DOJ, while competitors were doing their best to take advantage, piling on and doing some eye-gouging in the pile-up, Gordon had said some supportive things about Microsoft and had even been willing to testify on Microsoft's behalf despite the fact that Microsoft's Windows security bundle competed with Symantec products. What a mensch!

Well, it turns out, Bill Gates appreciated loyalty, deeply. Now he wanted to throw Gordon a lifeline.

"You see," Jon explained, "Gordon's in a bit of a crisis."

That was a profound understatement. Gordon Eubanks of Symantec was accused by another competitor of stealing trade secrets. That "crime" happens to be a felony in California, with a sentence of up to eight years in the slammer. Now, if you live in Silicon Valley, you will recognize that litigation is often deemed a marketing tool there. In those days and in some counties in and around the tech heartland, a private company could actually pay a county prosecutor to investigate an alleged competitive infraction. It would be like the Packers paying the referees in a playoff game against the Seahawks. It's almost a joke. *Almost*. But a felony is never a laughing matter.

The particulars wouldn't exactly drive the plot of a John Grisham thriller: Gordon had interviewed one of the competitor's marketing executives at that executive's request. Said executive, apparently wanting to impress Gordon with his strategic chops, had e-mailed a couple of the marketing memos he'd done for the competitor. To make the whole thing a little more mysterious (more Erle Stanley "Perry Mason" Gardner than Grisham), the memos were on an e-mail account attached to a laptop in the trunk of Gordon's car. Indeed, the e-mails and memos in question had never been downloaded. That didn't change the fact that the memos contained what the competitor alleged were the ingredients to the competitor's secret sauce. And it didn't change the prosecutors' contention that a felony had been committed in the theft of vital trade secrets.

While the charges were specious, Gordon proactively secured Allen Ruby as his attorney, unquestionably the finest defense lawyer on the planet and very likely in the solar system, too. Corporate lawyers generally develop a reputation as "Dr. No." Their general advice is, *No, don't do it. Keep it zipped. Duck and cover.* They want to do the talking, which means crisis is most often met with silence, which sounds like stonewalling, which doesn't wash with the public and even less with employees. Stonewalling means the company's operations actually calcify. Everything comes to a cement-wall stop.

Allen Ruby is no Dr. No. On the contrary, he understands the need to play offense. The material facts of almost any crisis are most often resolved with little *direct* damage. It's the *collateral* damage to the business, the business's relationships and its culture, that take the hit as the competitor's trash talk goes unanswered and pokes ding after ding into the organization's reputation. And in no business is reputation more important than in the digital security business.

Allen's attitude was that the show must go on. That, truly, is the lawyers' job: playing 325-pound pass protectors in a two-minute offensive drill.

His first question to Gordon and to us, as Gordon's advisers, was, "What do you want to say?"

He didn't want to try to wave us off from it, but rather to figure out what it would take to make a reputation-saving answer possible.

This is what we said was possible: We developed a 3x5 card message for Symantec's employees, friends, customers, and the press that did not ignore the charges, but ran right at them and over them. The message stated the innocence of the CEO and company unequivocally. In doing so, the message also conveyed Symantec's basic relevance and differentiation in the marketplace. Far from simply protesting innocence, the 3x5 card messaging included a concise marketing message for Symantec's products. It said this: *Symantec is winning in the marketplace and will win in court.*

Lest you think that "3x5 card" is a figure of speech, we had the suckers laminated. Employees *asked* for them, rather than waiting for management to hand them out. We found that most of them taped the card to their desk, close to computer keyboard and telephone. Rather than feeling lost in the dark, which is the way most employees feel when their company is in a crisis, they felt they

were helping to spread the light. The same was true of their suppliers, shareholders, board of directors, Hard Support customers,
and friends in the marketplace—all of whom received cards.

As the wheels of justice spun in place like those of a Yugo pant-
ing up Beacon Hill in February, Symantec kept charging forward.

As for the case, it was eventually dropped, as it should have
been. The reasons tap into an even more amazing bit of Allen
Ruby lore, but we worry that Scott County, California, might
judge revealing them a felony in their book, which would not be
so good for ours. So let's leave it at four big lessons:

1. Communicate and keep communicating inside out.
2. Tell your story.
3. Keep marketing aggressively.
4. Hire Allen Ruby.

Business crises can be deadly serious—although for most
companies they are relatively rare. This is in marked contrast to
the political campaign, in which every day is a crisis, even in a
run-of-the-mill campaign for a middle-of-the-road shoo-in candidate. A sense of urgency drives every day and wakes you up in the
middle of every night. If a campaign doesn't feel like a crisis, that
can only mean it no longer has a pulse and therefore no longer has
a chance of winning. Of course, campaigns also have their own
crises within the ongoing crisis. In our office, we have a framed
telegram transmitted one fated Sunday morning in 1988: "Hart
for President campaign meeting postponed. Details to follow."

Few readers under the age of forty will remember much about
the promising young, and handsome, senator from Colorado, but
you probably will remember the good ship *Monkey Business* and
maybe the name Donna Rice. People won't soon forget Texas
Governor Rick Perry's forgetting the third of his big three presidential priorities during the 2012 debates. ("The third one is ...
oops.") We suspect that Hispanics will long remember Donald

Trump's statements about Mexico sending its drug dealers and rapists across our border. Yeah, sure, "the Media" distorted his words. But that is what "the Media" always does, which is precisely why a crisis is not the time to run, hide, and lie low. It's the time to ensure that your message trumps (feeble pun regrettably intended) all others.

Then, too, there are the insurgent political campaigns we have been a part of worldwide: Aquino, Havel, Kim, Park, Fox, Yeltsin, Walesa, Shagari, and Obama, for instance. Globally, these usually create a crisis by winning democratic elections against autocrats who don't have any intention of giving up power.

Game Time

Step 9 is about crisis—not about crisis "management," but about crisis as game time, the time when all about you are losing their heads. Some, literally.

Sure, just like the big "crisis practice" law firms and PR shops, we love the tow truck rates that get charged in a crisis. But we love even more all the chances to put our insurgent principles to work. Game time is show time—when corporate managers not only listen to, but actually adopt our advice.

We take a different approach to crisis. We never talk about crisis management. Managing a crisis just ups the hourly rates of those law and PR firms we admittedly envy when we're in a greedy mood. *Managing* means *hunkering down* in a *defensive* position. As we witness any besieged politician endure successive press conferences, it becomes clear that *managing* crisis usually means *prolonging* crisis in a process that most often stumbles along a timeline from what the crisis experts Dawar and Pillutla have described as "unambiguous stonewalling to unambiguous support." It generally goes like this: No comment. No comment. Cannot be reached for comment. Deny, deny, deny, make a statement including, "we are sorry if some people were offended ..." stall, stall, stall, deny, deny, deny, settle, then make grim-faced statement including, "put this behind us."

Why "Manage" a Crisis When You Can *Win* a Crisis?

Like crisis itself, *managing* crisis sucks. We much prefer *winning* a crisis.

It is, after all, a contest. It is a campaign in itself. So we talk about defining success. We talk about re-mapping the battlefield. We talk about changing the dialogue. We talk about finding the opportunity hiding inside or obscured by the crisis of the moment. Ladies and gentlemen, please check to see that your seatbelts are tightly fastened. We may encounter a little rough air.

In our turbulent information environment, in which news reporting is in equal parts aggressive and shoddy, business crises take on the communications character of a political campaign. If you don't think there's a crisis simmering somewhere in your operations, well, think again, and then think some more. Someone with a Twitter feed is trying to find it, or, if possible, light it up.

It's true that very few political campaigns deal effectively with crisis. In a more compressed and sweaty process, most campaigns in crisis go through the same stumbles as businesses do. It is a headlong process punctuated by the teary press conference featuring stalwart spouse by the side of the senator/CEO turned perp: "I've disappointed my family and my church."

You can buy books (thousands of them) devoted entirely to crisis, but from our experience, all that you actually need is what you will find right here, in Step 9. These are the cut-to-the-T-bone basics learned with a lot of gray hair to show for the education. These are about preventing, neutralizing, and, most of all, winning in crisis situations.

The Steps

The steps toward actually winning a crisis? Here they are:

- ✪ Do a pre-crisis audit.
- ✪ Define your values and responsibilities.
- ✪ Map the battlefield 3D x 360 degrees.
- ✪ Presearch, research, and conduct an ongoing stakeholder dialogue.
- ✪ Develop a core strategy group.
- ✪ Define success, define the win.
- ✪ Define a core strategy.
- ✪ Create 3x5 card messaging.
- ✪ Communicate inside-out, early and often.
- ✪ Activate your Hard Support and your Soft Support. (*Su guerra es mi guerra.*)
- ✪ Change the dialogue, control the dialogue, and never let go.
- ✪ Tell the truth and tell it well.

Do a Pre-crisis Audit

Crises come in all varieties: a "rogue trader" pushing the envelope too far, a product that breaks or makes people sick, an environmental hazard that spills into the environment, a DUI for the CEO. No matter how diverse, most crises have a common cause. Maybe you remember the famous Strother Martin line from the movie *Cool Hand Luke*: "What we have here, is failure to communicate."

Somebody knew there was a problem brewing, a problem designed into the product. Someone knew a guy at the trading desk was going over the line. Somebody knew the CEO was living on the edge. Somebody knew, but nobody said. Complex organizations, silo organizations, and highly bureaucratic organizations with thick black lines at the top of the org chart encourage people toward greater loyalty to the small group than to those in the next silo, or the next line up the organization, or the organization as a whole. It's a dangerous pre-crisis (as in pre-cancerous) situation. And it's critically important to identify critical issues before the explosion.

We come from politics, but we're still not cynical about politics, about the process. We honestly and earnestly believe in democracy, and we believe that democracy is a dialogue. We believe that some democracy is a good thing, more democracy is better, and fluid democracy, a highly interactive conversation, is best of all.

A highly interactive conversation: *that's* what you want to achieve in your organization. It starts on the executive floor. More precisely, it starts with eliminating the executive floor and the polo field–sized corner office with the Remington sculptures, LeRoy Neiman paintings, and coffee table books that celebrate the Architecture of Headquarters.

Flat offices lead to flat organizations, which lead to open dialogue. (Just saying.) Steven Jobs famously designed Apple's Pixar's offices so that trips to the bathroom or break room forced people to walk from their department past other departments. Steven's Macintosh offices in the 1980s were the first with ping pong, musical instruments strewn about, video games, and a cooler full of free juices and water. (That cooler and its contents were the first things former PepsiCo CEO John Sculley eliminated when he took over as CEO of Apple.) If you're a leader, make time to walk and talk. This truly is the "walking the talk" of leadership communications. It is about conversations, not speeches. But, then, every speech should also be a conversation.

The best crisis is the one that never happens. Or as Churchill put it: "There is no greater feeling than to have been shot at with no effect." He wrote this in the same South African military campaign as his "nothing sharpens the mind" observation.

Crisis implies surprise and sudden shock to the system. If you hate surprises (as you really should), your first step is to be aware of pre-crisis conditions. This requires an audit we call an "everything communicates" audit, because of the key fact that every detail is important to some important stakeholder group and should be shaped around your core communications strategy.

Some crises can be prevented altogether. Others cannot be prevented, but they can be predicted. So find the organizational valves that cut off communications and open them up now. Here is what we mean: There are natural pre-crisis conditions present in all businesses. Lawyers and California city councilors put warning labels on as many of them as possible: "Please Don't Slam Your Head Into This Wall." Be assured that your business presents analogous conditions that are the likely points of potential pitfalls. Your insurance companies do audits of some of them before they write you a policy. For your own audit, it is extremely important to transfer ownership of the process to everyone in your company. Share ownership of all discovered pre-crisis conditions with the people in your company at all levels, from loading dock to boardroom.

As we've said, they already *know* where the next crisis will be born. Make sure they have incentives to let *you* know, too. According to Jack Ewing for the *New York Times*, Hans-Dieter Pötsch, the chairman of Volkswagen's supervisory board, said this: "There was a tolerance for breaking the rules" ("VW Says Emissions Cheating Was Not a One-Time Error," Dec. 10, 2015). Managers like to imply that VW-sized problems start with rogue employees and bubble up to the surface over time. Our experience is that these problems always develop in an atmosphere that permeates the company's air conditioning from the executive floor down to the factory floor. Management winks at stretching the truth. Management develops a history of unreliability with employees, suppliers, analysts, shareholders, and customers. That four-hour wait you once upon a time endured for the Comcast service call wasn't the result of some perverse and unpredictable decision of the service person or their dispatcher. Undoubtedly, the problem started in the office of the head bean counter. Everybody, or almost everybody knew about the structural strategic problem. Everybody, or almost everybody knew it was poisoning the relationship with customers everywhere. And everybody, or almost everybody in the company was talking about it. The problem was, nobody was listening. A little friction with customer service soon turned into a late-night TV joke and a problem for the corporate reputation that cost tens of millions to rectify.

The problems are being talked about somewhere in your company. The pre-crisis audit finds out where.

We once worked with the mining giant Rio Tinto. It was their custom to start every meeting with a "safety share," in which meeting participants were asked to share a thought about safety. It might be a tip from home, from commuting, business travel, or from their far-flung operations—mining ores that covered most of the Periodic Table of the Elements. The point was to keep safety at the front of every meeting and every mind.

Think like a veteran airline pilot. What *can* go wrong probably will. Don't fear it. Be ready for it. Anticipate it. Prepare for it.

Define your values and responsibilities

When Johnson & Johnson first began selling its shares to the public in 1944, its CEO and son of one of the founders, Robert Wood Johnson, experienced the kind of panic later common to entrepreneurs like Jobs, Gates, Page, and Brin. He was worried that this sudden wealth falling on the company and its employees would cause them to lose their way. So he sat down to think about it, and then he wrote about it, penning the company's celebrated manifesto, "Our Credo," which we discussed in Step 3. It is still inscribed on the wall in the waiting area of every office, on the first slide of every PowerPoint presentation, on the website, and in the annual report. A copy is framed on office walls and captured on desktops in Lucite. It's no mere token. Even though they have been a client, we can objectively say that the people of J&J believe the Credo and they live the Credo. Current CEO Alex Gorsky, only the seventh CEO since 1944, says, "If we take care of the Credo, everything else will take care of itself."

Walmart still tries to live the customer-focused values of Sam Walton, and McDonald's still follows many of Ray Kroc's views of the business as dependent upon the mutual needs and respect of the "three-legged stool: franchisees, employees, suppliers." Through Bill Gates's tenure as CEO of Microsoft, the company accepted its part in a revolution to improve work lives and home lives by executing a simple mission statement Gates himself had written: "A computer on every desk, in every home." (BTW: When Gates wrote this sentence, Microsoft didn't make computers. Not a one.)

Most often a start-up will accept the values of its founder, usually informally, but sometimes formally. For instance, the mission and values of founder Howard Schultz shape the Starbucks brand experience. You can find them on the Starbucks website. More importantly, you will feel them in almost every Starbucks store you walk into.

Our Mission

To inspire and nurture the human spirit—one person,
one cup and one neighborhood at a time.

Our Values

With our partners, our coffee and our customers at our
core, we live out these values:

Creating a culture of warmth and belonging, where everyone is welcome.

Acting with courage, challenging the status quo and finding new ways to grow our company and each other.

Being present, connecting with transparency, dignity and respect.

Delivering our very best in all we do, holding ourselves accountable for results.

We are performance driven, through the lens of humanity.

At Core Strategy Group, we have absorbed the principles of insurgency and embody them in this book. We believe these principles make work and life better. We use them in everything we do. And we go into any situation with our motto in mind: *Creo Merda Accidet.*

Define your responsibilities. Do it formally. Do it in longhand, like Robert Wood Johnson. Define your FIRST responsibilities (hint: buying a condo in Beaver Creek is not one of them). Bear in mind that, in defining the win (Step 2), you must define a win-win-win-win-win-win for you and all stakeholders: customers, employees, suppliers/partners, community, and shareholders.

Your company should also be clear in defining its values, at least as clear as Starbucks or Core Strategy Group.

What values shape decisions? Before you as CEO have the opportunity to define the company values, you must define them for yourself. What guides the decisions you make? What rules, what experiences or learning?

The principles of insurgency that we preach and practice and live have been learned through trial and error/trial and success. They have been learned through experience and observation.

Throughout, we never stop reviewing these principles or testing their validity. And, as we learn, we never stop refreshing them—while never changing the core ideas.

Map the battlefield 3D x 360 degrees

To a military strategist the battlefield is certainly a hostile environment, but it isn't an unfriendly one. In fact, it feels like home. And if you want to lead an enterprise these days, it had better start to feel like home to you, too.

The battlefield presents the four quadrants and four possibilities of SWOT:

strength (internal)	opportunity (external)
weakness (internal)	threat (external)

And it presents them in multiple dimensions, such as resources (or the lack thereof) and competitive advantages (or disadvantages). Obviously, you want to move to that upper-right quadrant, toward your internal strengths and the external market opportunities. You have to understand, too, the external market threats represented by competition, by market conditions, by supply chain, and by consumer perceptions and attitudes.

Remember, every battlefield presents a fluid situation, in which the only constant is change. Add to this: There are typically many battles in a war, just as there are many debates and primaries leading to a general election, and many market opportunities and challenges leading to success.

You must carefully assess the battlefield that is presented by a crisis. A given crisis may present objective problems, such as a toxic spill, a legal or ethical process, or a specific competitive threat. In addition, just about every crisis presents subjective problems, such as the changing perceptions, attitudes, and behavior of the Hard Opposition, Soft Opposition, Undecided, Soft Support, and Hard Support of any group arrayed upon the battlefield.

Having assessed the battlefield, you must map it both accurately and dynamically, since it will change as events move forward. The crisis that affects your company will create change in the marketplace, generating both challenge and opportunity. When we tell our clients to find the opportunity in a crisis, we're not just singing, "Look for the silver lining." Even when you are spinning in flames, you are changing the marketplace. Competitors will react. Consumers will react.

We remember a study Nike commissioned shortly after it launched the first Niketown megastore in Chicago. The reason for Niketown was that retailers had flat-out told Nike that selling apparel with the brand of an athletic shoe company would not work. There is no bigger threat than outright rejection of your product. But Nike accepted the threat as a challenge and decided to prove that it could create apparel lines using the same brand marketing model as they had used to sell athletic shoes.

Niketown, of course, has been a tremendous success—so tremendous that the very retailers who said the company couldn't sell Nike-branded apparel were now afraid that the apparel offered at Niketown would take business away from them. But the Nike study showed something remarkable. When a Niketown store opened, sales of Nike-branded products of all kinds rose in the area around that store. There were sales lifts in department stores, chain shoe stores, athletic equipment stores, and even mom 'n' pop shoe stores. Niketown was performing as a gushing fount of brand meaning, splashing out the imagery and appeal all over the local area. *What retailers had anticipated as a crisis of competition became a crisis of opportunity.*

Some crises are useful fictions. Everybody who strolls down Manhattan's Fifth Avenue is assaulted by GOING OUT OF BUSINESS signs. In a three-block space, you might pass four or five shops sporting such banners. The owners of these emporia know that consumers are highly likely to react to the *final* crisis of a business. So they create one.

The strange thing is, it's become a ritual. No New Yorker believes that any of these businesses are really going out of business. The routine has even been enshrined in a classic *New Yorker* cartoon: A proud papa stands in the doorway of a shop displaying the GOING OUT OF BUSINESS banner, looks at his little son, and proudly proclaims, "Someday, this will all be yours!"

Yes, these "going out of business" sales go on for decades. For decades, these final crises have continued to draw shoppers. And every day of those decades, the businesses with the "going out of business" signs have an effect on the retailers around them.

Some crises are works of nature. A rainstorm is a special crisis in Manhattan, as cabs vanish off the face of the Earth, and Uber starts up-charging. With the first drops that fall, umbrella salesmen materialize on every corner. "Ten dollah! Ten dollah!" is the cry—and the going price for a dollar's worth of spokes and fabric that *may* weather the next block or two.

There was a time when all of the West African immigrant umbrella sellers lived in the same downtown hotel, from which they fanned out to their corner spots when the clouds gathered. The crisis of ruining your new Jimmy Choo heels is the umbrella man's opportunity.

Your personal crisis creates opportunity for someone. All the idiot lights come on in your Lexus and the engine drops dead. *Mayday! Mayday! I'm going down ...* Your crisis is the tow truck driver's opportunity—and he (or she) will charge you accordingly.

Some crises *seem* to be dictated by the calendar. The sales that begin on Black Friday are apparently dictated by the calendar. In contrast to the perpetual fiction of the GOING OUT OF BUSINESS crisis, they have a basis in reality. Consumers assume it is the relentless reality of the calendar, but actually, their driver is the even more relentless internal cry that drives every retailer: *Everything must go!* From smallest boutique to biggest big box, unsold inventory presents a crisis. If the cry is *Everything must go!*, the ideal is *Everything must go at the highest possible margin.*

Every consumer knows that margin will begin to slide downward as Christmas Day nears. Today's savvy consumers play chicken with retailers, and they rely on FedEx, UPS, and (Lord help them) the United States Postal Service to give them the just-in-time edge in that game.

Come the holiday season, a sense of urgency intensifies on both the supply and consumption side of the retail equation. Moreover, the way sales at a Macy's or Amazon or Starbucks go in the unfolding course of the season, and the strategies and tactics these behemoths use, not only affect outcomes on their own battle-field—*their* customers, suppliers, distributors, and direct competitors—they shape the larger battlefield. An overall sense of urgency develops around *the* game, *the* toy, *the* book, *the* movie, *the* look, or *the* new flavor of this year's Christmas shopping season. Every merchant looks to the biggest incumbents as bellwethers. They want to see what shoppers elbow each other out of the way for.

Any massive sense of urgency generates a whole lot of stress—a feeling of imminent threat—but it also creates loads of opportunity that the "treasure hunt" strategies of a Gilt Groupe or a Costco exploit not just at Christmastime, but year-round.

A big part of the leadership campaign is converting crisis into opportunity. Good leaders instinctively respond to crisis

this way. **Great leaders create crises precisely so that they and their organizations can respond to them in this way.**

Interlude: The Whole Foods Story

Let's look at a combination of pre-crisis audit and battlefield mapping for Whole Foods Market.

Whole Foods Market was an insurgent brand that disrupted markets. Now it is being disrupted itself. Like many insurgent brands, Whole Foods Market not only invaded an existing category, it also helped create a category of its own. That's what Red Bull did with energy drinks and Tesla with luxury electric cars.

Great success can tempt any newly fat and happy leader to start thinking, planning, and acting like an incumbent, not an insurgent. The tendency to take the insurgent success for granted is developed with remarkable speed; and as it develops, so does the tendency to take customers for granted. When a leader and his or her business teeter-totter on the fulcrum at the intersection of *insurgency* and *incumbency*, the situation becomes "pre-crisis." And if this sounds to you disturbingly like the latex-gloved physician's diagnosis of "pre-cancerous," good. It should. Both situations can become rapidly fatal.

The early success of Whole Foods Market was propelled by the wave of consumer concern with over-processed foods, foods with long lists of unpronounceable ingredients, and the parallel rise of Italy's "slow food" movement and artisanal cooking, as well as by the farm-to-table revolution led by Alice Waters and Chez Panisse. The digital information environment sped and spread these changes, which created a shift in the American diet—beginning mainly within Gen X and wealthy Boomer communities and moving now into the mainstream of exurban and rural America.

Remember, incumbents hate change and begin by denying it. So the big food conglomerates, food retailers, and fast-food chains were very slow to accept this change. Even when they finally awakened, their toe-in-the-water strategies had them reacting by introducing superficial changes, mostly in flavors and ingredients. The core of their product offerings remained untouched and unchanged. Moreover, the mainstream incumbents did not take the seismic shift in diet seriously. They dismissed it as a marketing fad, and this, in the early years, gave Whole Foods Market and all the brands on its shelves even more running room.

What finally got the wholehearted, whole-headed attention of traditional food retail chains was not only the volume of customers being lured away as Whole Foods Market expanded, penetrating more and more territories, but also the much higher margins that Whole Foods Market was enjoying for the no-name natural and organic brands. Thanks to the level of trust established by Whole Foods Market's stringent standards—trust ratified by the notable absence of Big Food/Big Beverage brands on their shelves—the company was able to price higher. This stunned the supermarket incumbents, who had always operated on high volume with razor-thin margins. It was rather like the feeling the commander of a big army gets when guerrillas attack from the flank and rear: *This cannot be happening!*

The brilliance of Whole Foods insurgent marketing cannot be overstated. The company's dedication to little-known natural and organic brands not only positioned its brand effectively, it also re-positioned the opposition incumbent brands as the BIG FOOD status quo in which the status quo was defined as toxic or carcinogenic or both. Eat and die now or die later, but die.

Alas, while creating value through relevant differentiation—as a purveyor of natural, fresh, organic, healthy foods as opposed to the processed poison of the big food retailers—Whole Foods Market allowed a critical, possibly fatal, flaw to persist in their brand throughout the company's growth and success. This flaw was the perception that Whole Foods Market "over-charged." At first, the halo of trust successfully countered this perception, but, over the years, it began to gnaw through the halo. In fact, these days, it's not uncommon to hear, "Oh, you still shop at "Whole Paycheck"? And the reputation has become sufficiently entrenched to provide news media fodder for exposés by local news stations and for late-night talk show comics. When the stores started to put Asparagus Water—three stalks of a vegetable offered in a bottle containing water and priced at $6—on its shelves, it didn't help. Worse, the reputation for gouging became a part of the brand badge worn by its own customers. Once proud to be identified as discerning, they now felt themselves looking like saps, rubes, marks—whatever carnivals call their customers.

While Whole Foods suffered dangerous erosion of its hard-won brand, the major food retailers were finally waking up to the fundamental change that Whole Foods had been instrumental in fostering. The Big Food incumbents analyzed the core items consumers looked for in natural and organic versions. Over the years, these retailers had developed a "perimeter shopping strategy." It was pretty simple: you put the milk in the left-field corner, the bread in the right-field corner, and produce and deli at first base. The objective was to get people rolling around the store, rounding all the bases and, in the process, buying more than they had intended when they entered. Now, the big players analyzed key natural and organic brands, created their own natural and organic private-label brands, and began to place them strategically—just as they had always done with the basics of milk, bread, meat, produce, and deli.

The big-box brands also analyzed the situation, looking first at their customers. Walmart's "Wild Oats" brand not only offers customers the long-familiar basics, it has added an increasing variety of natural and organic products—which, and this is the disruption, it offers at the *same* prices it charges for the processed Big Food versions elsewhere in the stores.

Costco has also made a fundamental commitment to fresh, natural, and organic. And this spells real trouble for Whole Foods Market. Costco has become the smart badge brand for people who care about quality. In other words, following insurgent strategy flawlessly, both Walmart and Costco have used change to get control of the dialogue. Once challenged and repositioned by an insurgent Whole Foods, they have now positioned themselves as the insurgents and are repositioning an incumbent Whole Foods Market.

Outcome? Share prices of Whole Foods Market dropped by 50% in 2015. You want a crisis? *That* is a crisis. Full-blown. And it is one that certainly could have been anticipated and even headed off with a thorough pre-crisis audit and mapping of the competitive battlefield.

Presearch, Research, and Conduct an Ongoing Stakeholder Dialogue

The effect of crisis that matters most is how it changes the perceptions, attitudes, and behavior of consumers, employees, and other stakeholders—often including legislators, regulators, and the media.

We've said it again and again and again. You must be in continual dialogue with all stakeholder groups. Some of the dialogue can be personal and some can be carried out digitally. All of it must be fluid and interactive. Only the smallest companies can fully carry out the needed dialogue in face-to-face conversations. And in bigger organizations, presearch and research extend the reach of the conversation. Research is done in more than one way. Qualitative research is conducted through interviews and focus groups among representative individuals in your target groups. Quantitative research uses telephone or digital polling.

Presearch is our term for developing hypotheses to test potential and future scenarios with your target groups. Hypothesis testing isn't perfectly predictive, but it will guide you to create more hypotheses that begin to line up like Hansel and Gretel's breadcrumbs toward the best strategy.

Whichever technology or philosophy you adopt in developing research with internal or external groups, the one thing you must accept is the need to use research not only to provide you, the leader of the enterprise, with necessary information, but also to allow you to carry on a productive stakeholder dialogue by responding to what you hear. The action pattern is simple: Test, communicate, test, communicate.

Any research is better than no research, just as any level of democracy is better than no democracy. The ideal, however, is a fluid and never-ending dialogue. This gives you the opportunity to see trouble *before* it happens. And if there are table stakes for any claim to leadership, it's the ability to see the dog pile before you and your company are stepping in it.

Presearch and research are essential to accurately mapping the battlefield and to revising the map as the battlefield changes. These twin processes will allow you to do scenario planning that included the feedback needed to actually achieve the win you defined.

Develop a Core Strategy Group

We don't believe in hiding crises from employees, or, at least, from managers and company leaders. What can be known will be known, and the truth is much more powerful as propaganda than rumors, which are an irresistible force when the doors on the executive floor slam shut and managers whisper to each other in conference rooms.

Nevertheless, a crisis is not business as usual. Like any significant challenge or opportunity, making the most of the crisis situation requires the work of a diverse, talented, smart, and collaborative group of people. You want to represent 360 degrees of your organization's operations in this group, as Mike Roberts and Frank Vizcarra did with the McDonald's Noodle Team.

The core strategy group you create will own the definition of the win and the strategy that is derived from that definition. They will monitor and analyze the research and tune in to various listening posts up your supply chain as well as your demand chain. Assign a leader of the core strategy group who is not the CEO. The CEO shouldn't have to organize information or people. The CEO should be given room to listen, learn, and develop decisions.

We believe in war rooms, even though they have begun to become a bit of a cliché. Some companies have two or three operating at a time, and that dilutes both their meaning and power. A war room mentality is a focused mentality. Still, the technology now exists to create a virtual war room that keeps your core strategy group in communication securely and constantly. (Somebody please tell Hillary Clinton about this technology.) This way the team can be decentralized, as they will often have to be.

Define Success, Define the Win

Once you've understood the nature and extent of the crisis through triage informed by your pre-crisis audit, and once you've mapped the battlefield, you can define success. The question to be answered is *What are the acceptable and best outcomes?* As in any campaign—and, remember, we think any process in your business or career with an uncertain outcome constitutes a campaign—you must clearly define the win you want to go after.

Yes, it's important to be prudent and practical, as your chief counsel will constantly remind you.

No, you don't want to over-reach.

Still, you should define the win as more than "managing" the crisis. You want to end up with a win, not a managed crisis. So define that win in granular terms.

- ✪ How will the crisis productively and positively change the way key stakeholders feel, think, and behave toward you?
- ✪ How will the win change the "feel/think/do"?

Answer these questions, and you will have specified your desired outcome and destination. Now you can develop the strategy to attain it.

For projects and key challenges, you will always try to set an "Election Day" by which you must achieve the win you've defined. This is a lot harder with a crisis, though the crisis itself may have benchmark dates, such as a regulatory finding, a legal judgment, a report of the results of damage assessments, and even the tide of media reporting. As for the latter, it is well to remember that the media has its own cyclical movements. Reporters may herd together at the beginning of a news story, but eventually there will be the opportunity to develop a counter-story, a counter-narrative. This is considered a plum opportunity for any reporter—to break from the pack and develop a new story narrative. Obviously, you should be looking for that reporter and help develop the right counter-story for him or her.

Define a Core Strategy

The fact that you and your organization are in a crisis means you have lost control of the dialogue in some very important area of operations. Your core strategy must seek to regain control through change. And your strategy must precisely identify the votes you need to win. Again, you do this by segmenting all stakeholder audiences by attitude—HO SO Undecided SS HS—as discussed in Step 2.

Crisis strategy can change as events change the crisis battlefield. But it must be changed only by core strategy group decision, not by the fiat of the lawyers or the leader.

Create 3x5 Card Messaging

Develop your 3x5 card messaging out of your core strategy, with the central argument as the headline and four or five compelling support arguments as bullet points beneath this headline. Refresh yourself on this subject by giving Step 2 a second (or third) look.

Make sure to distribute the 3x5 card as widely as possible. It contains no lies or secret information. It is your public argument, and all those who want to support you or have an interest in supporting you should be armed with it. Of course, this 3x5 card message may change if events compel a change in the strategy. Until then, repeat, repeat, and repeat it.

Communicate Inside-Out, Early and Often

In your communications, consistency conveys conviction. It reinforces the strength of your arguments. The further those arguments move out from the leadership core toward employees, suppliers, market partners, distributors, Hard Support customers, and members of the media, legislators, and regulators, the more compelling they become. When those relevant experts who don't have a dog in the fight of the moment begin to reinforce your arguments, you are in a very strong position. Keep reinforcing the same messages. Keep communicating reinforcing information from objective sources, such as third-party analysts, the press, and so on. Make your supporters feel smart for supporting you.

Activate Your Hard Support and Soft Support (Su guerra es mi guerra)

Among those inside-out audiences, from employees to consumers, focus most intensively on Hard Support loyalists and your Soft Support. Both groups can be motivated to help broadcast your key themes and messages. In the case of Soft Support, you may have to entice them to tune into your communications before you can expect their help. Make everything you say and do relevant to them.

You will have an easier time with the Hard Support, who already have skin in the game. They have probably already expressed their loyalty to you. They identify with the brand. Whether employees or consumers, they will be the ones others go to for "inside" information. So, first and foremost, you want them to have the best and latest information. After all, in defending you they are also defending themselves and often their own self-interests. They want to pass on the best arguments in your favor. Make sure they have them at hand. Again, we have often printed *laminated* 3x5 cards for employees, suppliers, and key customers. And we have found that Hard Support individuals will put this card in a place that's handy for phone, e-mail, and social media. The further they are from your management, the more credible they will be in testimonials rendered on your behalf. And the more they are perceived to be objective third-party observers, the more powerful their testimony becomes.

The rule always is to support your supporters and manage your opposition.

Change the Dialogue, Control the Dialogue, and Never Let Go

The crisis may come on quickly, but the crisis situation often persists. As we've said, this crisis and how you and others respond to it will change the marketplace dialogue and affect all stake-holders. Expect several changes in the market dialogue through the weeks and months that the crisis and its after effects play out. Through it all, the objective remains the same: Never play defense. Always look for a way to play offense, even if the best (or only) opportunity to do so does not attack head-on the central issues of the crisis. Take the opportunity to act positively, affirmatively, and aggressively. The point is that your people and your support-ers will appreciate the change from dodging or catching the slings and arrows. It always feels better to deal a blow or two, even if they are not the deciding blows.

Something to bear in mind from today's political cam-paigns. Most of them in the United States cut to the chase and immediately begin with barrages and counter-barrages of negative TV commercials. Over the years, these negative ads have become less and less effective, to the point that they most frequently back-fire against the side that is launching the shot.

Even when you are counter-punching, be smart, not emotional. The information you present against your attackers must not only be true, it must also be perceived as relevant to the issues in play. No matter how delicious the fact you want to fire at your op-ponents, make sure it is seen as relevant to the stakeholders (the "voters") you need to move in order to get the win. Obviously, using an untruth when you're already on defense is strategically insane; it will turn even your supporters into doubters. Finally, any shot you fire must be objective, not personal. Those stake-holders, whether Soft Opposition or Soft Support, reject personal attacks. As they say in New Jersey, "Fuggedaboutit!"

Few battles are won with a single blow. But each blow you successfully land turns the battle in your favor by changing the dialogue and building the momentum. By defining the win, you define the outcome you ideally want. A crisis, however, creates a more fluid situation than what is found in most business-as-usual market environments. You may therefore find that outlining a series of "momentum wins" will provide easier objectives that will give your team and your supporters a real and powerful sense of momentum. Short of achieving instant victory—something that rarely happens to anybody anytime—nothing ends a crisis or turns it in your favor like the exhilarating sense of positive momentum.

While your "move the movable" focus in a crisis will naturally be on your Hard and Soft Support, you must not neglect the other end of the spectrum. Continually monitor and manage the opposition. The Hard Opposition will often overplay their hand during *your* crisis. But you must make sure the arguments of the Hard Opposition are not convincing and converting the Soft Opposition. You don't want the two to get together in one large opposition group. To prevent this, you have to find ways to divide and disrupt the Hard and Soft Opposition. Effectively and vigorously contest the claims of the Hard Opposition. Do everything you can—ethically and honestly—to refute them. At the very least, keep the Soft Opposition in doubt. They may remain (softly) opposed to you, but at least they won't have joined forces with those set firmly against you. That means they will sit out the battle.

Tell the Truth and Tell It Well

Of course you always want to communicate in the most glowing terms to create the most seductive narrative. That is a good goal—provided you always tell the truth. Conceal, prevaricate, dodge, weave, or lie, and you will find yourself screwed—and not in a good way. A lie will get you. As Rick Blaine put it in *Casablanca,* "Maybe not today, maybe not tomorrow, but soon, and for the rest of your life." The only damage greater than that created by silence and stonewalling is blurting out a lie.

Again, Henry Kissinger—whose boss, as you may recall, knew a thing or two about truth and its absence ("It's not the crime, it's the cover up")—once remarked of a certain line of argument that it was "elegant"—and "This has the added benefit of being true." We tell our candidates and corporate leaders much the same thing: "You will tell the truth eventually. The time it will help you most is at the beginning of the crisis. That's when you can use it to gain control of the dialogue."

Truth is a leader's most powerful campaign weapon. Tell the truth. Tell it fast. Tell it well.

⭐ Step 10 ⭐
LEADERSHIP, the Campaign

Do you really want to be a leader? We've just presented the model that works in today's turbulent markets and transparent information environment, and we hope you've already begun to incorporate what you've learned in Steps 1–9.

Not that they are enough.

Yes, we want to change what you do. We also want to change what you think and feel. We want to change your attitude. In this book, we've provided example after example taken from our experiences with great leaders in politics, business, sports, and the military. Over thirty-some years, we've learned how leaders think and act. We've learned the character and attitudes that support thought and action. More than any other single specific step, that's what we want for you. We want insurgent leadership to become your instinct. In professional sports, we hear a lot about a super-star's "instincts for the game." Those are learned. You can't learn fast-twitch muscles, brute strength, or a 41-inch vertical leap. But you can learn, as Wayne Gretzky learned, how to move to where the puck *will* be. That takes what Malcolm Gladwell defines as the ten thousand hours of practice. "Ten thousand hours" is an-other way of saying "champions are made, not born." Actually, many champions *are* born, only to be *unmade* through poor learn-ing and training or no learning and training. Take the time to *learn* the insurgent instinct. Get it into your blood.

In the heat of a football game, coaches yell to their players from the sidelines: "Finish it! Finish it!"

Finish it!

Finish this training. Make it your leadership checklist. Better yet, make it the core curriculum you use to teach those leaders who will come up after you. Teaching is always the best learning.

Here's the checklist of all ten steps. As you go through each step, turn or scroll back to the content and refresh your thinking about it. Internalize, then act. Create the muscle memory that discipline develops.

1. Decide to run: Decide to lead.
2. Think, plan, and act like an insurgent.
3. Gather your kitchen cabinet.
4. Prepare your campaign inside-out.
5. Announce your candidacy.
6. Define everything.
7. Control the dialogue.
8. Gain momentum.
9. Exploit crisis.
10. Rinse, repeat, and never stop running.

✪

Are you in? Good. Go to www.theleadershipcampaign.com. Outline the key components of your campaign. We'll pick three winners based solely on our opinions. The three winners win a six-hour campaign strategy meeting with Miller and Morey to finish your campaign in Washington, D.C.

Do you want to be a boss, or a leader? Great! Begin to answer these questions here or online.

- ✪ Name five leaders (politics, business, religion, education, science, military, entertainment).
- ✪ What one quality makes a great leader?
- ✪ Name one true leader you've worked with—and why.

Let's define the win for you. What is success?

- ✪ Six-month win
- ✪ Two-year win
- ✪ Five-year win
- ✪ Ten-year win
- ✪ Career win

Let's define the win for your company. What is success?

- ✪ Six-month win
- ✪ Two-year win
- ✪ Five-year win
- ✪ Ultimate win

What's changing in your business environment?

What needs to change in your company over the next two years?

What changes do you need to make in your style or the substance of your work?

Who's running against you? Name three.

Who the hell are you? We don't care what you've done; what we care about is how and why you did it. How do you decide big issues?

Why you? How are you going to deliver a win for ...

- ✪ Peers?
- ✪ Employees?
- ✪ Boss/CEO?
- ✪ Board of directors?
- ✪ Shareholders?
- ✪ Customers/Consumers?

Based on the situation you described for your organization (team or company), what is the change you represent?

What future do you represent for your organization and those groups above?

What does "do the doable" mean?

What does "move the movable" mean?

Within your organization ...

- ✪ Who is your Hard Opposition?
- ✪ Who is the Soft Opposition?
- ✪ Who is undecided?
- ✪ Who is the Soft Support?
- ✪ Who are your Hard Support loyalists?

Who are/have been your mentors in your career?

Who would you put in your fantasy kitchen cabinet (anybody in the world present or past)? Define the reason why for each one.

In your organization, who would you put on your core strategy group to meet the biggest challenge the company faces? Describe their qualities.

Given the change you say you represent and the win you say you will deliver, develop your 3x5 card:

_____HEADLINE_____

Support point #1

Support point #2

Support point #3

Support point #5

Crisis: A week after you have been named CEO, the company has been named by the FTC in a price-fixing investigation. You don't know anything about it. The press named the previous CEO as "under investigation." Your chief counsel says he thinks the charges are baseless, and, no matter what, you are in the clear personally.

What are the first three things you will do as leader?

1.

2.

3.

INDEX

ABOUT the Authors

Scott Miller

After graduating from Washington & Lee University, and a five-minute shot at the AFL, Scott Miller began work in advertising and then political consulting as Creative Director of McCann-Erickson in New York, where he led the creative work for such clients as Coca-Cola, Miller Brewing, Sony, L'Oreal, and many others. Mr. Miller won every major award for creative excellence in the advertising industry, including many Clio Awards and a Lion d'Or from the Cannes Film Festival.

In 1979 he founded Sawyer/Miller Group with David Sawyer. This strategic consulting group developed communications strategy for many political campaigns, corporations, and institutions. Among Sawyer/Miller Group's clients: Corazon Aquino,

Vaclav Havel, Coca-Cola, Microsoft, Miller Brewing, Boris Yeltsin, Drexel Burnham Lambert, Kim Dae Jung, Goldman-Sachs, Apple Computer, Virgilio Barco, USA for Africa/Hands Across America, Lech Walesa, and The Better World Foundation. Sawyer/Miller also advised over 40 U.S. candidates for Governor or Senator and several Presidential campaigns.

Steven Jobs of Apple Computer hired Sawyer/Miller in the 1980s. He asked for a strategy for their competition with IBM and Microsoft based on the insurgent strategic principles SMG was developing and learning in politics. That work with Apple created the strategic foundation for Scott's Core Strategy Group.

Over the past several years, he has worked on developing communications, marketing, and branding strategies for clients like McDonalds, Verizon, CitiGroup, Microsoft, Coca-Cola, Google, News Corp., Johnson & Johnson, Highfields Capital, Gannett, World Wildlife Fund, Rio Tinto, Cox Newspapers, Women & Co., Pepsico, The Newspaper Association of America, The Southern Company, American Express, The Home Depot, our Special Operations Military Command, and The Walt Disney Company.

He has continued his work in politics. In the 2004 U.S. election, Mr. Miller worked as a strategist for the Bush-Cheney campaign. In 2012 Scott founded RealLeader.com with Pat Caddell and Bob Perkins, and in 2013 with First Lady Michelle Obama's "Partnership for a Healthier America" initiative. During the 2014 elections, he founded "WeNeedSmith.com" and "A Promise to America" with Pat Caddell and Bob Perkins.

Mr. Miller provides commentary on political and corporate communications on the major television networks, and often lectures on communications, branding, and insurgent strategies. He wrote *Building Brandwidth* with Sergio Zyman, *The Underdog Advantage* with David Morey, and *One More Customer* with Fran Tarkenton. Former Editor of the Times of London James

Harding's book *Alpha Dogs* is based on Miller's work in politics. Scott is a member of the Council on Foreign Relations. He was included on several Who's Who lists over the years, before realizing the listing is basically a marketing scam. Nevertheless, to his great embarrassment, he bought one faux marble plaque.

Scott Miller lives in Atlanta, Georgia, with his wife Denise. His sons Tyler and Brett live in Brooklyn, New York.

David Morey

David Morey, Chairman and CEO of DMG Global and Vice Chairman of Core Strategy Group, is one of America's leading strategic consultants—and one of the nation's most sought-after speakers. Mr. Morey is the award-winning co-author of *The Underdog Advantage: Using the Power of Insurgent Strategy to Put Your Business on Top* (McGraw Hill), and *The Leadership Campaign: 10 Political Strategies to Win at Your Career and Propel Your Business to Victory* (Career Press 2016). He has worked with and helped add billions of dollars in revenue and market value to a wide range of Fortune 500 companies. Mr. Morey has worked with some of the world's top business leaders and he has advised five Nobel Peace Prize winners and 16 winning global presidential campaigns, including those of the 44th President of the United States, Barack Obama.

In politics, Mr. Morey has worked with foreign candidates and governments including: Colombian President Virgilio Barco; Philippine President Corazon Aquino; Russian President Boris Yeltsin, and The Dalai Lama. In 1997, he advised the winning presidential campaign of Kim Dae Jung, the first opposition leader to be elected in Korean history. Subsequently, he was an advisor to the Government of Korea during its financial crisis and recovery. More recently, Mr. Morey advised the successful campaigns of Vicente Fox, Mexico's first successful opposition presidential candidate in 70 years, and South Korea's Park Geun Hye.

In business, Mr. Morey has advised the senior officers of Fortune 100 entities and helped to launch a number of successful start-up companies and ventures. He has developed successful strategies for General Electric, Bancomer, Verizon, Apple, Samsung, Linkedin, Google, The Coca-Cola Company, Mars, KPMG, McDonald's, Microsoft, News Corp., Nike, Pepsi, P&G, Disney, Visa, American Express, TPG, and many others. For example, his strategic work over several years with Verizon and Coca-Cola helped to add over $100 billion to their market values, and his acquisition and turnaround strategies for Korea First Bank resulted in a quadrupling of profit for the private equity firm TPG.

Over the years, Mr. Morey has served as Adjunct Professor of International Affairs at Columbia University, specializing in global communications, and he currently teaches at the University of Pennsylvania. He was Chairman of the Council on Foreign Relations' Task Force on Public Diplomacy, Co-Chairman of the Fund For Peace and served on the Defense Science Board's Task Force on U.S. Strategic Communications and National Security. Mr. Morey was a four-time All-American Decathlon competitor, IC4A Champion, and a member of several U.S. national teams.

Mr. Morey was Foreign Policy Advisor to U.S. Senator John Glenn and a journalist in Eastern Europe and the Middle East. He studied at the Wharton School and Princeton University's Woodrow Wilson School, and was a Paul P. Harris scholar at the London School of Economics, where he received his Master's Degree with High Distinction. He has helped edit major books on a range of issues involving international politics, business and communications.